WORKERS OF ALL COUNTRIES, UNITE!

MAO TSE-TUNG

ON
LITERATURE AND ART

FOREIGN LANGUAGES PRESS
PEKING 1967

First Edition 1960
Second Edition (First Revised Translation) 1960
Third Edition (Second Revised Translation) 1967

Printed in the People's Republic of China

PUBLISHER'S NOTE

Comrade Mao Tse-tung is the greatest Marxist-Leninist of our era. He has inherited, defended and developed Marxism-Leninism with genius, creatively and comprehensively and has brought it to a higher and completely new stage. Mao Tse-tung's thought is Marxism-Leninism of the era in which imperialism is heading for total collapse and socialism is advancing to world-wide victory. It is the guiding principle for all the work of our Party and our country. This book contains Comrade Mao Tse-tung's "Talks at the Yenan Forum on Literature and Art" and other writings of his concerning culture and art. These brilliant contributions constitute the programme for the proletarian cultural revolution and the line for proletarian revolutionary literature and art, a programme and line which are most complete, thorough and correct. They embody the guiding principles for our cultural and art work and for the remoulding of the world outlook of intellectuals; they are the most powerful weapon for defeating modern revisionist ideology and all the different kinds of bourgeois ideology in the field of literature and art.

The English translation of *Mao Tse-tung on Literature and Art* which we published in 1960 was based on the first Chinese edition put out by the People's Literature Publishing House, Peking, in December 1958. The present English translation is based on the new Chinese edition put out by the same publishing house in June 1966 and contains one additional article, "Speech at the Chinese Communist Party's National Conference on Propaganda Work". The contents are arranged in chronological order except for "Talks at the Yenan Forum on Literature and Art", which appears first. Most of the titles are those of the original articles, chapters or sub-sections. But the following four titles have been supplied by the editor of the Chinese edition: "Myth and Reality", "The Chief Concern of China's Cultural Movement", "What to Praise and What to Condemn" and "On Literary Style".

CONTENTS

TALKS AT THE YENAN FORUM
ON LITERATURE AND ART

May 1942

INTRODUCTION

May 2, 1942

Comrades! You have been invited to this forum today
to exchange ideas and examine the relationship between work
in the literary and artistic fields and revolutionary work in
general. Our aim is to ensure that revolutionary literature
and art follow the correct path of development and provide
better help to other revolutionary work in facilitating the
overthrow of our national enemy and the accomplishment of
the task of national liberation.

In our struggle for the liberation of the Chinese people
there are various fronts, among which there are the fronts
of the pen and of the gun, the cultural and the military fronts.
To defeat the enemy we must rely primarily on the army
with guns. But this army alone is not enough; we must also
have a cultural army, which is absolutely indispensable for
uniting our own ranks and defeating the enemy. Since the
May 4th Movement[1] such a cultural army has taken shape in
China, and it has helped the Chinese revolution, gradually
reduced the domain of China's feudal culture and of the comprador culture which serves imperialist aggression, and weak-

ened their influence. To oppose the new culture the Chinese reactionaries can now only "pit quantity against quality". In other words, reactionaries have money, and though they can produce nothing good, they can go all out and produce in quantity. Literature and art have been an important and successful part of the cultural front since the May 4th Movement. During the ten years' civil war, the revolutionary literature and art movement grew greatly. That movement and the revolutionary war both headed in the same general direction, but these two fraternal armies were not linked together in their practical work because the reactionaries had cut them off from each other. It is very good that since the outbreak of the War of Resistance Against Japan, more and more revolutionary writers and artists have been coming to Yenan and our other anti-Japanese base areas. But it does not necessarily follow that, having come to the base areas, they have already integrated themselves completely with the masses of the people here. The two must be completely integrated if we are to push ahead with our revolutionary work. The purpose of our meeting today is precisely to ensure that literature and art fit well into the whole revolutionary machine as a component part, that they operate as powerful weapons for uniting and educating the people and for attacking and destroying the enemy, and that they help the people fight the enemy with one heart and one mind. What are the problems that must be solved to achieve this objective? I think they are the problems of the class stand of the writers and artists, their attitude, their audience, their work and their study.

The problem of class stand. Our stand is that of the proletariat and of the masses. For members of the Communist Party, this means keeping to the stand of the Party, keeping to Party spirit and Party policy. Are there any of our literary and art workers who are still mistaken or not clear in their understanding of this problem? I think there are. Many of our comrades have frequently departed from the correct stand.

The problem of attitude. From one's stand there follow specific attitudes towards specific matters. For instance, is one to extol or to expose? This is a question of attitude. Which attitude is wanted? I would say both. The question is, whom are you dealing with? There are three kinds of persons, the enemy, our allies in the united front and our own people; the last are the masses and their vanguard. We need to adopt a different attitude towards each of the three. With regard to the enemy, that is, Japanese imperialism and all the other enemies of the people, the task of revolutionary writers and artists is to expose their duplicity and cruelty and at the same time to point out the inevitability of their defeat, so as to encourage the anti-Japanese army and people to fight staunchly with one heart and one mind for their overthrow. With regard to our different allies in the united front, our attitude should be one of both alliance and criticism, and there should be different kinds of alliance and different kinds of criticism. We support them in their resistance to Japan and praise them for any achievement. But if they are not active in the War of Resistance, we should criticize them. If anyone opposes the Communist Party and the people and keeps moving down the path of reaction, we will firmly oppose him. As for the masses of the people, their toil and their struggle, their army and their Party, we should certainly praise them. The people, too, have their shortcomings. Among the proletariat many retain petty-bourgeois ideas, while both the peasants and the urban petty bourgeoisie have

3

backward ideas; these are burdens hampering them in their struggle. We should be patient and spend a long time in educating them and helping them to get these loads off their backs and combat their own shortcomings and errors, so that they can advance with great strides. They have remoulded themselves in struggle or are doing so, and our literature and art should depict this process. As long as they do not persist in their errors, we should not dwell on their negative side and consequently make the mistake of ridiculing them or, worse still, of being hostile to them. Our writings should help them to unite, to make progress, to press ahead with one heart and one mind, to discard what is backward and develop what is revolutionary, and should certainly not do the opposite.

The problem of audience, *i.e.,* the people for whom our works of literature and art are produced. In the Shensi-Kansu-Ningsia Border Region[2] and the anti-Japanese base areas of northern and central China, this problem differs from that in the Kuomintang areas, and differs still more from that in Shanghai before the War of Resistance. In the Shanghai period, the audience for works of revolutionary literature and art consisted mainly of a section of the students, office workers and shop assistants. After the outbreak of the War of Resistance the audience in the Kuomintang areas became somewhat wider, but it still consisted mainly of the same kind of people because the government there prevented the workers, peasants and soldiers from having access to revolutionary literature and art. In our base areas the situation is entirely different. Here the audience for works of literature and art consists of workers, peasants, soldiers and revolutionary cadres. There are students in the base areas, too, but they are different from students of the old type; they are either former or future cadres. The cadres of all types, fighters in the army, workers in the factories and peasants in the villages all want to read books and newspapers once they become literate, and those who are illiterate want to see plays and operas, look at drawings and paintings, sing songs and hear music; they are the audience for our works of literature and art. Take the cadres alone. Do not think they are few; they far outnumber the readers of any book published in the Kuomintang areas. There, an edition usually runs to only 2,000 copies, and even three editions add up to only 6,000; but as for the cadres in the base areas, in Yenan alone there are more than 10,000 who read books. Many of them, moreover, are tempered revolutionaries of long standing, who have come from all parts of the country and will go out to work in different places, so it is very important to do educational work among them. Our literary and art workers must do a good job in this respect.

Since the audience for our literature and art consists of workers, peasants and soldiers and of their cadres, the problem arises of understanding them and knowing them well. A great deal of work has to be done in order to understand them and know them well, to understand and know well all the different kinds of people and phenomena in the Party and government organizations, in the villages and factories and in the Eighth Route and New Fourth Armies. Our writers and artists have their literary and art work to do, but their primary task is to understand people and know them well. In this regard, how have matters stood with our writers and artists? I would say they have been lacking in knowledge and understanding; they have been like "a hero with no place to display his prowess". What does lacking in knowledge mean? Not knowing people well. The writers and artists do not have a good knowledge either of those whom they describe or of their audience; indeed they may hardly know them at all. They do not know the workers or peasants or soldiers well, and do not know the cadres well either. What does lacking in understanding mean? Not understanding the language, that is, not being familiar with the rich, lively language of the masses. Since many writers and artists stand aloof from the masses and lead empty lives, naturally they are unfamiliar with the language of the people. Accordingly, their works are not only insipid in language but often contain nondescript expressions of their own coining which run counter to popular usage. Many comrades like to talk about "a mass style". But what does it really mean? It means that the thoughts and feelings of our writers and artists should be fused with those of the masses of workers, peasants and soldiers. To achieve this fusion, they should conscientiously learn the language of the masses. How can you talk of literary and artistic creation if you find the very language of the masses largely incomprehensible? By "a hero with no place to display his prowess", we mean that your collection of great truths is not appreciated by the masses. The more you put on the airs of a veteran before the masses and play the "hero", the more you try to peddle such stuff to the masses, the less likely they are to accept it. If you want the masses to understand you, if you want to be one with the masses, you must make up your mind to undergo a long and even painful process of tempering. Here I might mention the experience of how my own feelings changed. I began life as a student and at school acquired the ways of a student; I then used to feel it undignified to do even a little manual labour, such as carrying my own luggage in the presence of my fellow students, who were incapable of carry-

6

ing anything, either on their shoulders or in their hands. At that time I felt that intellectuals were the only clean people in the world, while in comparison workers and peasants were dirty. I did not mind wearing the clothes of other intellectuals, believing them clean, but I would not put on clothes belonging to a worker or peasant, believing them dirty. But after I became a revolutionary and lived with workers and peasants and with soldiers of the revolutionary army, I gradually came to know them well, and they gradually came to know me well too. It was then, and only then, that I fundamentally changed the bourgeois and petty-bourgeois feelings implanted in me in the bourgeois schools. I came to feel that compared with the workers and peasants the unremoulded intellectuals were not clean and that, in the last analysis, the workers and peasants were the cleanest people and, even though their hands were soiled and their feet smeared with cow-dung, they were really cleaner than the bourgeois and petty-bourgeois intellectuals. That is what is meant by a change in feelings, a change from one class to another. If our writers and artists who come from the intelligentsia want their works to be well received by the masses, they must change and remould their thinking and their feelings. Without such a change, without such remoulding, they can do nothing well and will be misfits.

The last problem is study, by which I mean the study of Marxism-Leninism and of society. Anyone who considers himself a revolutionary Marxist writer, and especially any writer who is a member of the Communist Party, must have a knowledge of Marxism-Leninism. At present, however, some comrades are lacking in the basic concepts of Marxism. For instance, it is a basic Marxist concept that being determines consciousness, that the objective realities of class struggle and national struggle determine our thoughts and feelings. But some of our comrades turn this upside down and maintain that everything ought to start from "love". Now as for love, in a class society there can be only class love; but these comrades are seeking a love transcending classes, love in the abstract and also freedom in the abstract, truth in the abstract, human nature in the abstract, etc. This shows that they have been very deeply influenced by the bourgeoisie. They should thoroughly rid themselves of this influence and modestly study Marxism-Leninism. It is right for writers and artists to study literary and artistic creation, but the science of Marxism-Leninism must be studied by all revolutionaries, writers and artists not excepted. Writers and artists should study society, that is to say, should study the various classes in society, their mutual relations and respective conditions, their physiognomy and their psychology. Only when we grasp all this clearly can we have a literature and art that is rich in content and correct in orientation.

I am merely raising these problems today by way of introduction; I hope all of you will express your views on these and other relevant problems.

CONCLUSION
May 23, 1942

Comrades! Our forum has had three meetings this month. In the pursuit of truth we have carried on spirited debates in which scores of Party and non-Party comrades have spoken, laying bare the issues and making them more concrete. This, I believe, will very much benefit the whole literary and artistic movement.

In discussing a problem, we should start from reality and not from definitions. We would be following a wrong method if we first looked up definitions of literature and art in textbooks and then used them to determine the guiding principles for the present-day literary and artistic movement and to judge the different opinions and controversies that arise today. We are Marxists, and Marxism teaches that in our approach to a problem we should start from objective facts, not from abstract definitions, and that we should derive our guiding principles, policies and measures from an analysis of these facts. We should do the same in our present discussion of literary and artistic work.

What are the facts at present? The facts are: the War of Resistance Against Japan which China has been fighting for five years; the world-wide anti-fascist war; the vacillations of China's big landlord class and big bourgeoisie in the War of Resistance and their policy of high-handed oppression of the people; the revolutionary movement in literature and art since the May 4th Movement — its great contributions to the revolution during the last twenty-three years and its many shortcomings; the anti-Japanese democratic base areas of the Eighth Route and New Fourth Armies and the integration of large numbers of writers and artists with these armies and with the workers and peasants in these areas; the difference in both environment and tasks between the writers and artists in the base areas and those in the Kuomintang areas; and the controversial issues concerning literature and art which have arisen in Yenan and the other anti-Japanese base areas. These are the actual, undeniable facts in the light of which we have to consider our problems.

What then is the crux of the matter? In my opinion, it consists fundamentally of the problems of working for the masses and how to work for the masses. Unless these two problems are solved, or solved properly, our writers and artists will be ill-adapted to their environment and their tasks and will come up against a series of difficulties from without and within. My concluding remarks will centre on these two problems and also touch upon some related ones.

I

The first problem is: literature and art for whom?

This problem was solved long ago by Marxists, especially by Lenin. As far back as 1905 Lenin pointed out emphatically that our literature and art should "serve . . . the millions and tens of millions of working people".[3] For comrades engaged in literary and artistic work in the anti-Japanese base areas it might seem that this problem is already solved and needs no further discussion. Actually, that is not the case. Many comrades have not found a clear solution. Consequently their sentiments, their works, their actions and their views on the guiding principles for literature and art have inevitably been more or less at variance with the needs of the masses and of the practical struggle. Of course, among the numerous men of culture, writers, artists and other literary and artistic workers engaged in the great struggle for liberation together with the Communist Party and the Eighth Route and New Fourth Armies, a few may be careerists who are with us only temporarily, but the overwhelming majority are working energetically for the common cause. By relying on these comrades, we have achieved a great deal in our literature, drama, music and fine arts. Many of these writers and artists have begun their work since the outbreak of the War of Resistance; many others did much revolutionary work before the war, endured many hardships and influenced broad masses of the people by their activities and works. Why do we say, then, that even among these comrades there are some who have not reached a clear solution of the problem of whom literature and art are for? Is it conceivable that there are still some who maintain that revolutionary literature and art are not for the masses of the people but for the exploiters and oppressors?

Indeed literature and art exist which are for the exploiters and oppressors. Literature and art for the landlord class are feudal literature and art. Such were the literature and art of the ruling class in China's feudal era. To this day such literature and art still have considerable influence in China. Literature and art for the bourgeoisie are bourgeois literature and art. People like Liang Shih-chiu,[4] whom Lu Hsun criticized, talk about literature and art as transcending classes, but in fact they uphold bourgeois literature and art and oppose proletarian literature and art. Then literature and art exist which serve the imperialists — for example, the works of Chou Tso-jen, Chang Tzu-ping[5] and their like — which we call traitor literature and art. With us, literature and art are for the people, not for any of the above groups. We have said that China's new culture at the present stage is an anti-imperialist, anti-feudal culture of the masses of the people under the leadership of the proletariat. Today, anything that is truly of the masses must necessarily be led by the proletariat. Whatever is under the leadership of the bourgeoisie cannot possibly be of the masses. Naturally, the same applies to the new literature and art which are part of the new culture. We should take over the rich legacy and the good traditions in literature and art that have been handed down from past ages in China and foreign countries, but the aim must still be to serve the masses of the people. Nor do we refuse to utilize the literary and artistic forms of the past, but in our hands these old forms, remoulded and infused with new content, also become something revolutionary in the service of the people.

Who, then, are the masses of the people? The broadest sections of the people, constituting more than 90 per cent of our total population, are the workers, peasants, soldiers and urban petty bourgeoisie. Therefore, our literature and art are first for the workers, the class that leads the revolution. Secondly, they are for the peasants, the most numerous and most steadfast of our allies in the revolution. Thirdly, they are for the armed workers and peasants, namely, the Eighth Route and New Fourth Armies and the other armed units of the people, which are the main forces of the revolutionary war. Fourthly, they are for the labouring masses of the urban petty bourgeoisie and for the petty-bourgeois intellectuals, both of whom are also our allies in the revolution and capable of long-term co-operation with us. These four kinds of people constitute the overwhelming majority of the Chinese nation, the broadest masses of the people.

Our literature and art should be for the four kinds of people we have enumerated. To serve them, we must take the class stand of the proletariat and not that of the petty bourgeoisie. Today, writers who cling to an individualist, petty-bourgeois stand cannot truly serve the masses of revolutionary workers, peasants and soldiers. Their interest is mainly focused on the small number of petty-bourgeois intellectuals. This is the crucial reason why some of our comrades cannot correctly solve the problem of "for whom?" In saying this I am not referring to theory. In theory, or in words, no one in our ranks regards the masses of workers, peasants and soldiers as less important than the petty-bourgeois intellectuals. I am referring to practice, to action. In practice, in action, do they regard petty-bourgeois intellectuals as more important than workers, peasants and soldiers? I think they do. Many comrades concern themselves with studying the petty-bourgeois intellectuals and analysing their psychology, and they concentrate on portraying these intellectuals and excusing or defending their shortcomings, instead of guiding the intellectuals to join with them in getting closer to the masses of workers, peasants and soldiers, taking part in the practical struggles of the masses, portraying and educating the masses. Coming from the petty bourgeoisie and being themselves intellectuals, many comrades seek friends only among intellectuals and concentrate on studying and describing them. Such study and description are proper if done from a proletarian position. But that is not what they do, or not what they do fully. They take the petty-bourgeois stand and produce works that are the self-expression of the petty bourgeoisie, as can be seen in quite a number of literary and artistic products. Often they show heartfelt sympathy for intellectuals of petty-bourgeois origin, to the extent of sympathizing with or even praising their shortcomings. On the other hand, these comrades seldom come into contact with the masses of workers, peasants and soldiers, do not understand or study them, do not have intimate friends among them and are not good at portraying them; when they do depict them, the clothes are the clothes of working people but the faces are those of petty-bourgeois intellectuals. In certain respects they are fond of the workers, peasants and soldiers and the cadres stemming from them; but there are times when they do not like them and there are some respects in which they do not like them: they do not like their feelings or their manner or their nascent literature and art (the wall newspapers, murals, folk songs, folk tales, etc.). At times they are fond of these things too, but that is when they are hunting for novelty, for something with which to embellish their own works, or even for certain backward features. At other times they openly despise these things and are partial to what belongs to the petty-bourgeois intellectuals or even to the bourgeoisie. These comrades have their feet planted on the side of the petty-bourgeois intellectuals; or, to put it more elegantly, their innermost soul is still a kingdom of the petty-bourgeois intelligentsia. Thus they have not yet solved, or not yet clearly solved, the problem of "for whom?" This applies not only to newcomers to Yenan; even among comrades who have been to the front and worked for a number of years in our base areas and in the Eighth Route and New Fourth Armies, many have not completely solved this problem. It requires a long period of time, at least eight or ten years, to solve it thoroughly. But however long it takes, solve it we must and solve it unequivocally and thoroughly. Our literary and art workers must accomplish this task and shift their stand; they must gradually move their feet over to the side of the workers, peasants and soldiers, to the side of the proletariat, through the process of going into their very midst and into the thick of practical struggles and through the process of studying Marxism and society. Only in this way can we have a literature and art that are truly for the workers, peasants and soldiers, a truly proletarian literature and art.

This question of "for whom?" is fundamental; it is a question of principle. The controversies and divergences, the opposition and disunity arising among some comrades in the past were not on this fundamental question of principle but on secondary questions, or even on issues involving no principle. On this question of principle, however, there has been hardly any divergence between the two contending sides and they have shown almost complete agreement; to some extent, both tend to look down upon the workers, peasants and soldiers and divorce themselves from the masses. I say "to some extent" because, generally speaking, these comrades do not look down upon the workers, peasants and soldiers or divorce themselves from the masses in the same way as the Kuomintang does. Nevertheless, the tendency is there. Unless this fundamental problem is solved, many other problems will not be easy to solve. Take, for instance, the sectarianism in literary and art circles. This too is a question of principle, but sectarianism can only be eradicated by putting forward and faithfully applying the slogans, "For the workers and peasants!", "For the Eighth Route and New Fourth Armies!" and "Go among the masses!" Otherwise the problem of sectarianism can never be solved. Lu Hsun once said:

A common aim is the prerequisite for a united front. . . . The fact that our front is not united shows that we have not been able to unify our aims, and that some people are working only for small groups or indeed only for themselves. If we all aim at serving the masses of workers and peasants, our front will of course be united.[6]

The problem existed then in Shanghai; now it exists in Chungking too. In such places the problem can hardly be solved thoroughly, because the rulers oppress the revolutionary writers and artists and deny them the freedom to go out among the masses of workers, peasants and soldiers. Here with us the situation is entirely different. We encourage revolutionary writers and artists to be active in forming intimate contacts with the workers, peasants and soldiers, giving them complete freedom to go among the masses and to create a genuinely revolutionary literature and art. Therefore, here among us the problem is nearing solution. But nearing solution is not the same as a complete and thorough solution. We must study Marxism and study society, as we have been saying, precisely in order to achieve a complete and thorough solution. By Marxism we mean living Marxism which plays an effective role in the life and struggle of the masses, not Marxism in words. With Marxism in words transformed into Marxism in real life, there will be no more sectarianism. Not only will the problem of sectarianism be solved, but many other problems as well.

II

Having settled the problem of whom to serve, we come to the next problem, how to serve. To put it in the words of some of our comrades: should we devote ourselves to raising standards, or should we devote ourselves to popularization?

In the past, some comrades, to a certain or even a serious extent, belittled and neglected popularization and laid undue stress on raising standards. Stress should be laid on raising standards, but to do so one-sidedly and exclusively, to do so excessively, is a mistake. The lack of a clear solution to the problem of "for whom?", which I referred to earlier, also manifests itself in this connection. As these comrades are not clear on the problem of "for whom?", they have no correct criteria for the "raising of standards" and the "popularization" they speak of, and are naturally still less able to find the correct relationship between the two. Since our literature and art are basically for the workers, peasants and soldiers, "popularization" means to popularize among the workers, peasants and soldiers, and "raising standards" means to advance from their present level. What should we popularize among them? Popularize what is needed and can be readily accepted by the feudal landlord class? Popularize what is needed and can be readily accepted by the bourgeoisie? Popularize what is needed and can be readily accepted by the petty-bourgeois intellectuals? No, none of these will do. We must popularize only what is needed and can be readily accepted by the workers, peasants and soldiers themselves. Consequently, prior to the task of educating the workers, peasants and soldiers, there is the task of learning from them. This is even more true of raising standards. There must be a basis from which to raise. Take a bucket of water, for instance; where is it to be raised from if not from the ground? From mid-air? From what basis, then, are literature and art to be raised? From the basis of the feudal classes? From the basis of the bourgeoisie? From the basis of the petty-bourgeois intellectuals? No, not from any of these; only from the basis of the masses of workers, peasants and soldiers. Nor does this mean raising the workers, peasants and soldiers to the "heights" of the feudal classes, the bourgeoisie or the petty-bourgeois intellectuals; it means raising the level of literature and art in the direction in which the workers, peasants and soldiers are themselves advancing, in the direction in which the proletariat is advancing. Here again the task of learning from the workers, peasants and soldiers comes in. Only by starting from the workers, peasants and soldiers can we have a correct understanding of popularization and of the raising of standards and find the proper relationship between the two.

In the last analysis, what is the source of all literature and art? Works of literature and art, as ideological forms, are products of the reflection in the human brain of the life of a given society. Revolutionary literature and art are the products of the reflection of the life of the people in the brains of revolutionary writers and artists. The life of the people is always a mine of the raw materials for literature and art, materials in their natural form, materials that are crude, but most vital, rich and fundamental; they make all literature and art seem pallid by comparison; they provide literature and art with an inexhaustible source, their only source. They are the only source, for there can be no other. Some may ask, is there not another source in books, in the literature and art of ancient times and of foreign countries? In fact, the literary and artistic works of the past are not a source but a stream; they were created by our predecessors and the foreigners out of the literary and artistic raw materials they found in the life of the people of their time and place. We must take over all the fine things in our literary and artistic heritage, critically assimilate whatever is beneficial, and use them as examples when we create works out of the literary and artistic raw materials in the life of the people of our own time and place. It makes a difference whether or not we have such examples, the difference between crudeness and refinement, between roughness and polish, between a low and a high level, and between slower and faster work. Therefore, we must on no account reject the legacies of the ancients and the foreigners or refuse to learn from them, even though they are the works of the feudal or bourgeois classes. But taking over legacies and using them as examples must never replace our own creative work; nothing can do that. Uncritical transplantation or copying from the ancients and the foreigners is the most sterile and harmful dogmatism in literature and art. China's revolutionary writers and artists, writers and artists of promise, must go among the masses; they must for a long period of time unreservedly and wholeheartedly go among the masses of workers, peasants and soldiers, go into the heat of the struggle, go to the only source, the broadest and richest source, in order to observe, experience, study and analyse all the different kinds of people, all the classes, all the masses, all the vivid patterns of life and struggle, all the raw materials of literature and art. Only then can they proceed to creative work. Otherwise, you will have nothing to work with and you will be nothing but a phoney writer or artist, the kind that Lu Hsun in his will so earnestly cautioned his son never to become.[7]

Although man's social life is the only source of literature and art and is incomparably livelier and richer in content, the people are not satisfied with life alone and demand literature and art as well. Why? Because, while both are beautiful, life as reflected in works of literature and art can and ought to be on a higher plane, more intense, more concentrated, more typical, nearer the ideal, and therefore more universal than actual everyday life. Revolutionary literature and art should create a variety of characters out of real life and help the masses to propel history forward. For example, there is suffering from hunger, cold and oppression on the one hand, and exploitation and oppression of man by man on the other. These facts exist everywhere and people look upon them as commonplace. Writers and artists concentrate such everyday phenomena, typify the contradictions and struggles within them and produce works which awaken the masses, fire them with enthusiasm and impel them to unite and struggle to transform their environment. Without such literature and art, this task could not be fulfilled, or at least not so effectively and speedily.

What is meant by popularizing and by raising standards in works of literature and art? What is the relationship between these two tasks? Popular works are simpler and plainer, and therefore more readily accepted by the broad masses of the people today. Works of a higher quality, being more polished, are more difficult to produce and in general do not circulate so easily and quickly among the masses at present. The problem facing the workers, peasants and soldiers is this: they are now engaged in a bitter and bloody struggle with the enemy but are illiterate and uneducated as a result of long years of rule by the feudal and bourgeois classes, and therefore they are eagerly demanding enlightenment, education and works of literature and art which meet their urgent needs and which are easy to absorb, in order to heighten their enthusiasm in struggle and confidence in victory, strengthen their unity and fight the enemy with one heart and one mind. For them the prime need is not "more flowers on the brocade" but "fuel in snowy weather". In present conditions, therefore, popularization is the more pressing task. It is wrong to belittle or neglect popularization.

Nevertheless, no hard and fast line can be drawn between popularization and the raising of standards. Not only is it possible to popularize some works of higher quality even now, but the cultural level of the broad masses is steadily rising. If popularization remains at the same level for ever, with the same stuff being supplied month after month and year after year, always the same "Little Cowherd"[8] and the same "man, hand, mouth, knife, cow, goat",[9] will not the educators and those being educated be six of one and half a dozen of the other? What would be the sense of such popularization?

The people demand popularization and, following that, higher standards; they demand higher standards month by month and year by year. Here popularization means popularizing for the people and raising of standards means raising the level for the people. And such raising is not from mid-air, or behind closed doors, but is actually based on popularization. It is determined by and at the same time guides popularization. In China as a whole the development of the revolution and of revolutionary culture is uneven and their spread is gradual. While in one place there is popularization and then raising of standards on the basis of popularization, in other places popularization has not even begun. Hence good experience in popularization leading to higher standards in one locality can be applied in other localities and serve to guide popularization and the raising of standards there, saving many twists and turns along the road. Internationally, the good experience of foreign countries, and especially Soviet experience, can also serve to guide us. With us, therefore, the raising of standards is based on popularization, while popularization is guided by the raising of standards. Precisely for this reason, so far from being an obstacle to the raising of standards, the work of popularization we are speaking of supplies the basis for the work of raising standards which we are now doing on a limited scale, and prepares the necessary conditions for us to raise standards in the future on a much broader scale.

Besides such raising of standards as meets the needs of the masses directly, there is the kind which meets their needs indirectly, that is, the kind which is needed by the cadres. The cadres are the advanced elements of the masses and generally have received more education; literature and art of a higher level are entirely necessary for them. To ignore this would be a mistake. Whatever is done for the cadres is also entirely for the masses, because it is only through the cadres that we can educate and guide the masses. If we go against this aim, if what we give the cadres cannot help them educate and guide the masses, our work of raising standards will be like shooting at random and will depart from the fundamental principle of serving the masses of the people.

To sum up: through the creative labour of revolutionary writers and artists, the raw materials found in the life of the people are shaped into the ideological form of literature and art serving the masses of the people. Included here are the more advanced literature and art as developed on the basis of elementary literature and art and as required by those sections of the masses whose level has been raised, or, more immediately, by the cadres among the masses. Also included here are elementary literature and art which, conversely, are guided by more advanced literature and art and are needed primarily by the overwhelming majority of the masses at present. Whether more advanced or elementary, all our literature and art are for the masses of the people, and in the first place for the workers, peasants and soldiers; they are created for the workers, peasants and soldiers and are for their use.

Now that we have settled the problem of the relationship between the raising of standards and popularization, that of the relationship between the specialists and the popularizers can also be settled. Our specialists are not only for the cadres, but also, and indeed chiefly, for the masses. Our specialists in literature should pay attention to the wall newspapers of the masses and to the reportage written in the army and the villages. Our specialists in drama should pay attention to the small troupes in the army and the villages. Our specialists in music should pay attention to the songs of the masses. Our specialists in the fine arts should pay attention to the fine arts of the masses. All these comrades should make close contact with comrades engaged in the work of popularizing literature and art among the masses. On the one hand, they should help and guide the popularizers, and on the other, they should learn from these comrades and, through them, draw nourishment from the masses to replenish and enrich themselves so that their specialities do not become "ivory towers", detached from the masses and from reality and devoid of content or life. We should esteem the specialists, for they are very valuable to our cause. But we should tell them that no revolutionary writer or artist can do any meaningful work unless he is closely linked with the masses, gives expression to their thoughts and feelings and serves them as a loyal spokesman. Only by speaking for the masses can he educate them and only by being their pupil can he be their teacher. If he regards himself as their master, as an aristocrat who lords it over the "lower orders", then, no matter how talented he may be, he will not be needed by the masses and his work will have no future.

Is this attitude of ours utilitarian? Materialists do not oppose utilitarianism in general but the utilitarianism of the feudal, bourgeois and petty-bourgeois classes; they oppose those hypocrites who attack utilitarianism in words but in deeds embrace the most selfish and short-sighted utilitarianism. There is no "ism" in the world that transcends utilitarian considerations; in class society there can be only the utilitarianism of this or that class. We are proletarian revolutionary utilitarians and take as our point of departure the unity of the present and future interests of the broadest masses, who constitute over 90 per cent of the population; hence we are revolutionary utilitarians aiming for the broadest and the most long-range objectives, not narrow utilitarians concerned only with the partial and the immediate. If, for instance, you reproach the masses for their utilitarianism and yet for your own utility, or that of a narrow clique, force on the market and propagandize among the masses a work which pleases only the few but is useless or even harmful to the majority, then you are not only insulting the masses but also revealing your own lack of self-knowledge. A thing is good only when it brings real benefit to the masses of the people. Your work may be as good as "The Spring Snow", but if for the time being it caters only to the few and the masses are still singing the "Song of the Rustic Poor",[10] you will get nowhere by simply scolding them instead of trying to raise their level. The question now is to bring about a unity between "The Spring Snow" and the "Song of the Rustic Poor", between higher standards and popularization. Without such a unity, the highest art of any expert cannot help being utilitarian in the narrowest sense; you may call this art "pure and lofty" but that is merely your own name for it which the masses will not endorse.

Once we have solved the problems of fundamental policy, of serving the workers, peasants and soldiers and of how to serve them, such other problems as whether to write about the bright or the dark side of life and the problem of unity will also be solved. If everyone agrees on the fundamental policy, it should be adhered to by all our workers, all our schools, publications and organizations in the field of literature and art and in all our literary and artistic activities. It is wrong to depart from this policy and anything at variance with it must be duly corrected.

III

Since our literature and art are for the masses of the people, we can proceed to discuss a problem of inner-Party relations, *i.e.*, the relation between the Party's work in literature and art and the Party's work as a whole, and in addition a problem of the Party's external relations, *i.e.*, the relation between the Party's work in literature and art and the work of non-Party people in this field, a problem of the united front in literary and art circles.

Let us consider the first problem. In the world today all culture, all literature and art belong to definite classes and are geared to definite political lines. There is in fact no such thing as art for art's sake, art that stands above classes or art that is detached from or independent of politics. Proletarian literature and art are part of the whole proletarian revolutionary cause; they are, as Lenin said, cogs and wheels[11] in the whole revolutionary machine. Therefore, Party work in literature and art occupies a definite and assigned position in Party revolutionary work as a whole and is subordinated to the revolutionary tasks set by the Party in a given revolutionary period. Opposition to this arrangement is certain to lead to dualism or pluralism, and in essence amounts to "politics — Marxist, art — bourgeois", as with Trotsky. We do not favour overstressing the importance of literature and art, but neither do we favour underestimating their importance. Literature and art are subordinate to politics, but in their turn exert a great influence on politics. Revolutionary literature and art are part of the whole revolutionary cause, they are cogs and wheels in it, and though in comparison with certain other and more important parts they may be less significant and less urgent and may occupy a secondary position, nevertheless, they are indispensable cogs and wheels in the whole machine, an indispensable part of the entire revolutionary cause. If we had no literature and art even in the broadest and most ordinary sense, we could not carry on the revolutionary movement and win victory. Failure to recognize this is wrong. Furthermore, when we say that literature and art are subordinate to politics, we mean class politics, the politics of the masses, not the politics of a few so-called statesmen. Politics, whether revolutionary or counter-revolutionary, is the struggle of class against class, not the activity of a few individuals. The revolutionary struggle on the ideological and artistic fronts must be subordinate to the political struggle because only through politics can the needs of the class and the masses find expression in concentrated form. Revolutionary statesmen, the political specialists who know the science or art of revolutionary politics, are simply the leaders of millions upon millions of statesmen — the masses. Their task is to collect the opinions of these mass statesmen, sift and refine them, and return them to the masses, who then take them and put them into practice. They are therefore not the kind of aristocratic "statesmen" who work behind closed doors and fancy they have a monopoly of wisdom. Herein lies the difference in principle between proletarian statesmen and decadent bourgeois statesmen. This is precisely why there can be complete unity between the political character of our literary and artistic works and their truthfulness. It would be wrong to fail to realize this and to debase the politics and the statesmen of the proletariat.

Let us consider next the question of the united front in the world of literature and art. Since literature and art are subordinate to politics and since the fundamental problem in China's politics today is resistance to Japan, our Party writers and artists must in the first place unite on this issue of resistance to Japan with all non-Party writers and artists (ranging from Party sympathizers and petty-bourgeois writers and artists to all those writers and artists of the bourgeois and landlord classes who are in favour of resistance to Japan). Secondly, we should unite with them on the issue of democracy. On this issue there is a section of anti-Japanese writers and artists who do not agree with us, so the range of unity will unavoidably be somewhat more limited. Thirdly, we should unite with them on issues peculiar to the literary and artistic world, questions of method and style in literature and art; here again, as we are for socialist realism and some people do not agree, the range of unity will be narrower still. While on one issue there is unity, on another there is struggle, there is criticism. The issues are at once separate and interrelated, so that even on the very ones which give rise to unity, such as resistance to Japan, there are at the same time struggle and criticism. In a united front, "all unity and no struggle" and "all struggle and no unity" are both wrong policies — as with the Right capitulationism and tailism, or the "Left" exclusivism and sectarianism, practised by some comrades in the past. This is as true in literature and art as in politics.

The petty-bourgeois writers and artists constitute an important force among the forces of the united front in literary and art circles in China. There are many shortcomings in both their thinking and their works, but, comparatively speaking, they are inclined towards the revolution and are close to the working people. Therefore, it is an especially important task to help them overcome their shortcomings and to win them over to the front which serves the working people.

27

Literary and art criticism is one of the principal methods of struggle in the world of literature and art. It should be developed and, as comrades have rightly pointed out, our past work in this respect has been quite inadequate. Literary and art criticism is a complex question which requires a great deal of special study. Here I shall concentrate only on the basic problem of criteria in criticism. I shall also comment briefly on a few specific problems raised by some comrades and on certain incorrect views.

In literary and art criticism there are two criteria, the political and the artistic. According to the political criterion, everything is good that is helpful to unity and resistance to Japan, that encourages the masses to be of one heart and one mind, that opposes retrogression and promotes progress; on the other hand, everything is bad that is detrimental to unity and resistance to Japan, foments dissension and discord among the masses and opposes progress and drags people back. How can we tell the good from the bad — by the motive (the subjective intention) or by the effect (social practice)? Idealists stress motive and ignore effect, while mechanical materialists stress effect and ignore motive. In contradistinction to both, we dialectical materialists insist on the unity of motive and effect. The motive of serving the masses is inseparably linked with the effect of winning their approval; the two must be united. The motive of serving the individual or a small clique is not good, nor is it good to have the motive of serving the masses without the effect of winning their approval and benefiting them. In examining the subjective intention of a writer or artist, that is, whether his motive is correct and good, we do not judge by his declarations but by the effect of his actions (mainly his works) on the masses in society. The criterion for judging subjective intention or motive is social practice and its effect. We want no sectarianism in our literary and art criticism and, subject to the general principle of unity for resistance to Japan, we should tolerate literary and art works with a variety of political attitudes. But at the same time, in our criticism we must adhere firmly to principle and severely criticize and repudiate all works of literature and art expressing views in opposition to the nation, to science, to the masses and to the Communist Party, because these so-called works of literature and art proceed from the motive and produce the effect of undermining unity for resistance to Japan. According to the artistic criterion, all works of a higher artistic quality are good or comparatively good, while those of a lower artistic quality are bad or comparatively bad. Here, too, of course, social effect must be taken into account. There is hardly a writer or artist who does not consider his own work beautiful, and our criticism ought to permit the free competition of all varieties of works of art; but it is also entirely necessary to subject these works to correct criticism according to the criteria of the science of aesthetics, so that art of a lower level can be gradually raised to a higher and art which does not meet the demands of the struggle of the broad masses can be transformed into art that does.

There is the political criterion and there is the artistic criterion; what is the relationship between the two? Politics cannot be equated with art, nor can a general world outlook be equated with a method of artistic creation and criticism. We deny not only that there is an abstract and absolutely unchangeable political criterion, but also that there is an abstract and absolutely unchangeable artistic criterion; each class in every class society has its own political and artistic criteria. But all classes in all class societies invariably put the political criterion first and the artistic criterion second. The bourgeoisie always shuts out proletarian literature and art, however great their artistic merit. The proletariat must similarly distinguish among the literary and art works of past ages and determine its attitude towards them only after examining their attitude to the people and whether or not they had any progressive significance historically. Some works which politically are downright reactionary may have a certain artistic quality. The more reactionary their content and the higher their artistic quality, the more poisonous they are to the people, and the more necessary it is to reject them. A common characteristic of the literature and art of all exploiting classes in their period of decline is the contradiction between their reactionary political content and their artistic form. What we demand is the unity of politics and art, the unity of content and form, the unity of revolutionary political content and the highest possible perfection of artistic form. Works of art which lack artistic quality have no force, however progressive they are politically. Therefore, we oppose both the tendency to produce works of art with a wrong political viewpoint and the tendency towards the "poster and slogan style" which is correct in political viewpoint but lacking in artistic power. On questions of literature and art we must carry on a struggle on two fronts.

Both these tendencies can be found in the thinking of many comrades. A good number of comrades tend to neglect artistic technique; it is therefore necessary to give attention to the raising of artistic standards. But as I see it, the political side is more of a problem at present. Some comrades lack elementary political knowledge and consequently have

30

all sorts of muddled ideas. Let me cite a few examples from Yenan.

"The theory of human nature." Is there such a thing as human nature? Of course there is. But there is only human nature in the concrete, no human nature in the abstract. In class society there is only human nature of a class character; there is no human nature above classes. We uphold the human nature of the proletariat and of the masses of the people, while the landlord and bourgeois classes uphold the human nature of their own classes, only they do not say so but make it out to be the only human nature in existence. The human nature boosted by certain petty-bourgeois intellectuals is also divorced from or opposed to the masses; what they call human nature is in essence nothing but bourgeois individualism, and so, in their eyes, proletarian human nature is contrary to human nature. "The theory of human nature" which some people in Yenan advocate as the basis of their so-called theory of literature and art puts the matter in just this way and is wholly wrong.

"The fundamental point of departure for literature and art is love, love of humanity." Now love may serve as a point of departure, but there is a more basic one. Love as an idea is a product of objective practice. Fundamentally, we do not start from ideas but from objective practice. Our writers and artists who come from the ranks of the intellectuals love the proletariat because society has made them feel that they and the proletariat share a common fate. We hate Japanese imperialism because Japanese imperialism oppresses us. There is absolutely no such thing in the world as love or hatred without reason or cause. As for the so-called love of humanity, there has been no such all-inclusive love since humanity was divided into classes. All the ruling classes of the past were fond of advocating it, and so were many so-called sages and wise men, but nobody has ever really practised it, because it is impossible in class society. There will be genuine love of humanity — after classes are eliminated all over the world. Classes have split society into many antagonistic groupings; there will be love of all humanity when classes are eliminated, but not now. We cannot love enemies, we cannot love social evils, our aim is to destroy them. This is common sense; can it be that some of our writers and artists still do not understand this?

"Literary and artistic works have always laid equal stress on the bright and the dark, half and half." This statement contains many muddled ideas. It is not true that literature and art have always done this. Many petty-bourgeois writers have never discovered the bright side. Their works only expose the dark and are known as the "literature of exposure". Some of their works simply specialize in preaching pessimism and world-weariness. On the other hand, Soviet literature in the period of socialist construction portrays mainly the bright. It, too, describes shortcomings in work and portrays negative characters, but this only serves as a contrast to bring out the brightness of the whole picture and is not on a so-called half-and-half basis. The writers and artists of the bourgeoisie in its period of reaction depict the revolutionary masses as mobs and themselves as saints, thus reversing the bright and the dark. Only truly revolutionary writers and artists can correctly solve the problem of whether to extol or to expose. All the dark forces harming the masses of the people must be exposed and all the revolutionary struggles of the masses of the people must be extolled; this is the fundamental task of revolutionary writers and artists.

"The task of literature and art has always been to expose." This assertion, like the previous one, arises from ignorance of the science of history. Literature and art, as we have shown, have never been devoted solely to exposure. For revolutionary writers and artists the targets for exposure can never be the masses, but only the aggressors, exploiters and oppressors and the evil influence they have on the people. The masses too have shortcomings, which should be overcome by criticism and self-criticism within the people's own ranks, and such criticism and self-criticism is also one of the most important tasks of literature and art. But this should not be regarded as any sort of "exposure of the people". As for the people, the question is basically one of education and of raising their level. Only counter-revolutionary writers and artists describe the people as "born fools" and the revolutionary masses as "tyrannical mobs".

"This is still the period of the satirical essay, and Lu Hsun's style of writing is still needed." Living under the rule of the dark forces and deprived of freedom of speech, Lu Hsun used burning satire and freezing irony, cast in the form of essays, to do battle; and he was entirely right. We, too, must hold up to sharp ridicule the fascists, the Chinese reactionaries and everything that harms the people; but in the Shensi-Kansu-Ningsia Border Region and the anti-Japanese base areas behind the enemy lines, where democracy and freedom are granted in full to the revolutionary writers and artists and withheld only from the counter-revolutionaries, the style of the essay should not simply be like Lu Hsun's. Here we can shout at the top of our voices and have no need for veiled and roundabout expressions, which are hard for the people to understand. When dealing with the people and not with their enemies, Lu Hsun never ridiculed or attacked the

revolutionary people and the revolutionary Party in his "satirical essay period", and these essays were entirely different in
manner from those directed against the enemy. To criticize
the people's shortcomings is necessary, as we have already
said, but in doing so we must truly take the stand of the
people and speak out of whole-hearted eagerness to protect
and educate them. To treat comrades like enemies is to go
over to the stand of the enemy. Are we then to abolish
satire? No. Satire is always necessary. But there are
several kinds of satire, each with a different attitude, satire
to deal with our enemies, satire to deal with our allies and
satire to deal with our own ranks. We are not opposed to
satire in general; what we must abolish is the abuse of satire.

"I am not given to praise and eulogy. The works of people
who eulogize what is bright are not necessarily great and the
works of those who depict the dark are not necessarily paltry." If you are a bourgeois writer or artist, you will eulogize
not the proletariat but the bourgeoisie, and if you are a proletarian writer or artist, you will eulogize not the bourgeoisie
but the proletariat and working people: it must be one or
the other. The works of the eulogists of the bourgeoisie are
not necessarily great, nor are the works of those who show
that the bourgeoisie is dark necessarily paltry; the works of
the eulogists of the proletariat are not necessarily not great,
but the works of those who depict the so-called "darkness" of
the proletariat are bound to be paltry — are these not facts of
history as regards literature and art? Why should we not
eulogize the people, the creators of the history of mankind?
Why should we not eulogize the proletariat, the Communist
Party, New Democracy and socialism? There is a type of
person who has no enthusiasm for the people's cause and

34

looks coldly from the side-lines at the struggles and victories of the proletariat and its vanguard; what he is interested in, and will never weary of eulogizing, is himself, plus perhaps a few figures in his small coterie. Of course, such petty-bourgeois individualists are unwilling to eulogize the deeds and virtues of the revolutionary people or heighten their courage in struggle and their confidence in victory. Persons of this type are merely termites in the revolutionary ranks; of course, the revolutionary people have no need for these "singers".

"It is not a question of stand; my class stand is correct, my intentions are good and I understand all right, but I am not good at expressing myself and so the effect turns out bad." I have already spoken about the dialectical materialist view of motive and effect. Now I want to ask, is not the question of effect one of stand? A person who acts solely by motive and does not inquire what effect his action will have is like a doctor who merely writes prescriptions but does not care how many patients die of them. Or take a polit-ical party which merely makes declarations but does not care whether they are carried out. It may well be asked, is this a correct stand? And is the intention here good? Of course, mistakes may occur even though the effect has been taken into account beforehand, but is the intention good when one continues in the same old rut after facts have proved that the effect is bad? In judging a party or a doctor, we must look at practice, at the effect. The same applies in judging a writer. A person with truly good intentions must take the effect into account, sum up experience and study the methods or, in creative work, study the technique of expres-sion. A person with truly good intentions must criticize the

35

shortcomings and mistakes in his own work with the utmost candour and resolve to correct them. This is precisely why Communists employ the method of self-criticism. This alone is the correct stand. Only in this process of serious and responsible practice is it possible gradually to understand what the correct stand is and gradually obtain a good grasp of it. If one does not move in this direction in practice, if there is simply the complacent assertion that one "understands all right", then in fact one has not understood at all.

"To call on us to study Marxism is to repeat the mistake of the dialectical materialist creative method, which will harm the creative mood." To study Marxism means to apply the dialectical materialist and historical materialist viewpoint in our observation of the world, of society and of literature and art; it does not mean writing philosophical lectures into our works of literature and art. Marxism embraces but cannot replace realism in literary and artistic creation, just as it embraces but cannot replace the atomic and electronic theories in physics. Empty, dry dogmatic formulas do indeed destroy the creative mood; not only that, they first destroy Marxism. Dogmatic "Marxism" is not Marxism, it is anti-Marxism. Then does not Marxism destroy the creative mood? Yes, it does. It definitely destroys creative moods that are feudal, bourgeois, petty-bourgeois, liberalistic, individualist, nihilist, art-for-art's sake, aristocratic, decadent or pessimistic, and every other creative mood that is alien to the masses of the people and to the proletariat. So far as proletarian writers and artists are concerned, should not these kinds of creative moods be destroyed? I think they should; they should be utterly destroyed. And while they are being destroyed, something new can be constructed.

V

The problems discussed here exist in our literary and art circles in Yenan. What does that show? It shows that wrong styles of work still exist to a serious extent in our literary and art circles and that there are still many defects among our comrades, such as idealism, dogmatism, empty illusions, empty talk, contempt for practice and aloofness from the masses, all of which call for an effective and serious campaign of rectification.

We have many comrades who are still not very clear on the difference between the proletariat and the petty bourgeoisie. There are many Party members who have joined the Communist Party organizationally but have not yet joined the Party wholly or at all ideologically. Those who have not joined the Party ideologically still carry a great deal of the muck of the exploiting classes in their heads, and have no idea at all of what proletarian ideology, or communism, or the Party is. "Proletarian ideology?" they think. "The same old stuff!" Little do they know that it is no easy matter to acquire this stuff. Some will never have the slightest Communist flavour about them as long as they live and can only end up by leaving the Party. Therefore, though the majority in our Party and in our ranks are clean and honest, we must in all seriousness put things in order both ideologically and organizationally if we are to develop the revolutionary movement more effectively and bring it to speedier success. To put things in order organizationally requires our first doing so ideologically, our launching a struggle of proletarian ideology against non-proletarian ideology. An ideological struggle is already under way in literary and art circles in Yenan, and it is most necessary. Intellectuals of

37

petty-bourgeois origin always stubbornly try in all sorts of ways, including literary and artistic ways, to project themselves and spread their views, and they want the Party and the world to be remoulded in their own image. In the circumstances it is our duty to jolt these "comrades" and tell them sharply, "That won't work! The proletariat cannot accommodate itself to you; to yield to you would actually be to yield to the big landlord class and the big bourgeoisie and to run the risk of undermining our Party and our country." Whom then must we yield to? We can mould the Party and the world only in the image of the proletarian vanguard. We hope our comrades in literary and art circles will realize the seriousness of this great debate and join actively in this struggle, so that every comrade may become sound and our entire ranks may become truly united and consolidated ideologically and organizationally.

Because of confusion in their thinking, many of our comrades are not quite able to draw a real distinction between our revolutionary base areas and the Kuomintang areas and they make many mistakes as a consequence. A good number of comrades have come here from the garrets of Shanghai, and in coming from those garrets to the revolutionary base areas, they have passed not only from one kind of place to another but from one historical epoch to another. One society is semi-feudal, semi-colonial, under the rule of the big landlords and big bourgeoisie, the other is a revolutionary new-democratic society under the leadership of the proletariat. To come to the revolutionary bases means to enter an epoch unprecedented in the thousands of years of Chinese history, an epoch in which the masses of the people wield state power. Here the people around us and the audience for our propaganda are totally different. The past epoch is gone, never to return. Therefore, we must integrate ourselves with the new masses without any hesitation. If, living among the new masses, some comrades, as I said before, are still "lacking in knowledge and understanding" and remain "heroes with no place to display their prowess", then difficulties will arise for them, and not only when they go out to the villages; right here in Yenan difficulties will arise for them. Some comrades may think, "Well, I had better continue writing for the readers in the Great Rear Area;[12] it is a job I know well and has 'national significance'." This idea is entirely wrong. The Great Rear Area is also changing. Readers there expect authors in the revolutionary base areas to tell about the new people and the new world and not to bore them with the same old tales. Therefore, the more a work is written for the masses in the revolutionary base areas, the more national significance will it have. Fadeyev in *The Debacle*[13] only told the story of a small guerrilla unit and had no intention of pandering to the palate of readers in the old world; yet the book has exerted world-wide influence. At any rate in China its influence is very great, as you know. China is moving forward, not back, and it is the revolutionary base areas, not any of the backward, retrogressive areas, that are leading China forward. This is a fundamental issue that, above all, comrades must come to understand in the rectification movement.

Since integration into the new epoch of the masses is essential, it is necessary thoroughly to solve the problem of the relationship between the individual and the masses. This couplet from a poem by Lu Hsun should be our motto:

Fierce-browed, I coolly defy a thousand pointing fingers,
Head-bowed, like a willing ox I serve the children.[14]

The "thousand pointing fingers" are our enemies, and we will never yield to them, no matter how ferocious. The "children" here symbolize the proletariat and the masses. All Communists, all revolutionaries, all revolutionary literary and art workers should learn from the example of Lu Hsun and be "oxen" for the proletariat and the masses, bending their backs to the task until their dying day. Intellectuals who want to integrate themselves with the masses, who want to serve the masses, must go through a process in which they and the masses come to know each other well. This process may, and certainly will, involve much pain and friction, but if you have the determination, you will be able to fulfil these requirements.

Today I have discussed only some of the problems of fundamental orientation for our literature and art movement; many specific problems remain which will require further study. I am confident that comrades here are determined to move in the direction indicated. I believe that in the course of the rectification movement and in the long period of study and work to come, you will surely be able to bring about a transformation in yourselves and in your works, to create many fine works which will be warmly welcomed by the masses of the people, and to advance the literature and art movement in the revolutionary base areas and throughout China to a glorious new stage.

NOTES

[1] The May 4th Movement was an anti-imperialist and anti-feudal revolutionary movement which began on May 4, 1919. In the first half of that year, the victors of World War I, *i.e.*, Britain, France, the United

States, Japan, Italy and other imperialist countries, met in Paris to divide the spoils and decided that Japan should take over all the privileges previously enjoyed by Germany in Shantung Province, China. The students of Peking were the first to show determined opposition to this scheme, holding rallies and demonstrations on May 4. The Northern warlord government arrested more than thirty students in an effort to suppress this opposition. In protest, the students of Peking went on strike and large numbers of students in other parts of the country responded. On June 3 the Northern warlord government started arresting students in Peking en masse, and within two days about a thousand were taken into custody. This aroused still greater indignation throughout the country. From June 5 onwards, the workers of Shanghai and many other cities went on strike and the merchants in these places shut their shops. Thus, what was at first a patriotic movement consisting mainly of intellectuals rapidly developed into a national patriotic movement embracing the proletariat, the urban petty bourgeoisie and the bourgeoisie. And along with the growth of this patriotic movement, the new cultural movement which had begun before May 4 as a movement against feudalism and for the promotion of science and democracy, grew into a vigorous and powerful revolutionary cultural movement whose main current was the propagation of Marxism-Leninism.

2 The Shensi-Kansu-Ningsia Border Region was the revolutionary base area which was gradually built up after 1931 through revolutionary guerrilla warfare in northern Shensi. When the Central Red Army arrived in northern Shensi after the Long March, it became the seat of the Central Committee of the Chinese Communist Party and the central base area of the revolution. The Shensi-Kansu-Ningsia Red Area was changed into the Shensi-Kansu-Ningsia Border Region after the formation of the Anti-Japanese National United Front in 1937. Nearly thirty counties, *i.e.*, Yenan, Fuhsien, Kanchuan, Yenchuan, Yenchang, Anting (now Tzechang), Ansai, Chihtan, Chingpien, Shenmu, Fuku, Tingpien, Hsunyi, Chunhua, Huanhsien, Chingyang, Hoshui, Chenyuan, Ninghsien, Chengning, Yenchih, Suiteh, Chingchien, Wupao, Michih, Chiahsien, etc., were under its jurisdiction.

3 See V. I. Lenin, "Party Organisation and Party Literature", in which he described the characteristics of proletarian literature as follows:

It will be a free literature, because the idea of socialism and sympathy with the working people, and not greed or careerism, will bring ever new forces to its ranks. It will be a free literature, because it will serve, not some satiated heroine, not the bored "upper ten thousand"

41

suffering from fatty degeneration, but the millions and tens of millions of working people — the flower of the country, its strength and its future. It will be a free literature, enriching the last word in the revolutionary thought of mankind with the experience and living work of the socialist proletariat, bringing about permanent interaction between the experience of the past (scientific socialism, the completion of the development of socialism from its primitive, utopian forms) and the experience of the present (the present struggle of the worker comrades). (*Collected Works*, Eng. ed., FLPH, Moscow, 1962, Vol. X, pp. 48-49.)

[4] Liang Shih-chiu, a member of the counter-revolutionary National Socialist Party, for a long time propagated reactionary American bourgeois ideas on literature and art. He stubbornly opposed the revolution and reviled revolutionary literature and art.

[5] Chou Tso-jen and Chang Tzu-ping capitulated to the Japanese aggressors after the Japanese occupied Peking and Shanghai in 1937.

[6] Lu Hsun, "My View on the League of Left-Wing Writers" in the collection *Two Hearts, Complete Works*, Chin. ed., 1957, Vol. IV.

[7] See Lu Hsun's essay, "Death", in the "Addenda", *The Last Collection of Essays Written in a Garret in the Quasi-Concession, Complete Works*, Chin. ed., 1958, Vol. VI.

[8] The "Little Cowherd" is a popular Chinese folk operetta with only two people acting in it, a cowherd and a village girl, who sing a question and answer duet. In the early days of the War of Resistance Against Japan, this form was used, with new words, for anti-Japanese propaganda and for a time found great favour with the public.

[9] The Chinese characters for these six words are written simply, with only a few strokes, and were usually included in the first lessons in old primers.

[10] "The Spring Snow" and the "Song of the Rustic Poor" were songs of the Kingdom of Chu in the 3rd century B.C. The music of the first was on a higher level than that of the second. As the story is told in "Sung Yu's Reply to the King of Chu" in Prince Chao Ming's *Anthology of Prose and Poetry*, when someone sang "The Spring Snow" in the Chu capital, only a few dozen people joined in, but when the "Song of the Rustic Poor" was sung, thousands did so.

[11] See V. I. Lenin, "Party Organisation and Party Literature": "Literature must become *part* of the common cause of the proletariat, 'a cog

and a screw' of one single great Social-Democratic mechanism set in motion by the entire politically-conscious vanguard of the entire working class." (*Collected Works*, Eng. ed., FLPH, Moscow, 1962, Vol. X, p. 45.)

[12] The Great Rear Area was the name given during the War of Resistance to the vast areas under Kuomintang control in southwestern and northwestern China which were not occupied by the Japanese invaders, as distinguished from the "small rear area", the anti-Japanese base areas behind the enemy lines under the leadership of the Communist Party.

[13] *The Debacle* by the famous Soviet writer Alexander Fadeyev was published in 1927 and translated into Chinese by Lu Hsun. The novel describes the struggle of a partisan detachment of workers, peasants and revolutionary intellectuals in Siberia against the counter-revolutionary brigands during the Soviet civil war.

[14] This couplet is from Lu Hsun's "In Mockery of Myself" in *The Collection Outside the Collection, Complete Works*, Chin. ed., 1958, Vol. VII.

THE MOVEMENT FOR EDUCATION

March 1927

In China education has always been the exclusive preserve of the landlords, and the peasants have had no access to it. But the landlords' culture is created by the peasants, for its sole source is the peasants' sweat and blood. In China 90 per cent of the people have had no education, and of these the overwhelming majority are peasants. The moment the power of the landlords was overthrown in the rural areas, the peasants' movement for education began. See how the peasants who hitherto detested the schools are today zealously setting up evening classes! They always disliked the "foreign-style school". In my student days, when I went back to the village and saw that the peasants were against the "foreign-style school", I, too, used to identify myself with the general run of "foreign-style students and teachers" and stand up for it, feeling that the peasants were somehow wrong. It was not until 1925, when I lived in the countryside for six months and was already a Communist and had acquired the Marxist viewpoint, that I realized I had been wrong and the peasants right. The texts used in the rural primary schools were entirely about urban things and unsuited to rural needs. Besides, the attitude of the primary school teachers towards the peasants was very bad and, far from being helpful to the peasants, they became objects of dislike. Hence the peasants preferred the old-style schools ("Chinese classes", as they called them) to the modern schools (which they called "foreign classes") and the old-style teachers to the ones in the primary schools. Now the peasants are enthusiastically establishing evening classes, which they call peasant schools. Some have already been opened, others are being organized, and on the average there is one school per township. The peasants are very enthusiastic about these schools, and regard them, and only them, as their own. The funds for the evening schools come from the "public revenue from superstition", from ancestral temple funds, and from other idle public funds or property. The county education boards wanted to use this money to establish primary schools, that is, "foreign-style schools" not suited to the needs of the peasants, while the latter wanted to use it for peasant schools, and the outcome of the dispute was that both got some of the money, though there are places where the peasants got it all. The development of the peasant movement has resulted in a rapid rise in their cultural level. Before long tens of thousands of schools will have sprung up in the villages throughout the province; this is quite different from the empty talk about "universal education", which the intelligentsia and the so-called "educationalists" have been bandying back and forth and which after all this time remains an empty phrase.

> From *Report on an Investigation of the Peasant Movement in Hunan*

MYTH AND REALITY

August 1937

... There are innumerable transformations in mythology, for instance, Kua Fu's race with the sun in *Shan Hai Ching*,[1] Yi's shooting down of nine suns in *Huai Nan Tzu*,[2] the Monkey King's seventy-two metamorphoses in *Hsi Yu Chi*,[3] the numerous episodes of ghosts and foxes metamorphosed into human beings in the *Strange Tales of Liao Chai*,[4] etc. But these legendary transformations of opposites are not concrete changes reflecting concrete contradictions. They are naive, imaginary, subjectively conceived transformations conjured up in men's minds by innumerable real and complex transformations of opposites into one another. Marx said, "All mythology masters and dominates and shapes the forces of nature in and through the imagination; hence it disappears as soon as man gains mastery over the forces of nature."[5] The myriads of changes in mythology (and also in nursery tales) delight people because they imaginatively picture man's conquest of the forces of nature, and the best myths possess "eternal charm", as Marx put it; but myths are not built out of the concrete contradictions existing in given conditions and therefore are not a scientific reflection of reality. That is to say, in myths or nursery tales the aspects constituting a contradiction have only an imaginary identity, not a concrete identity.

From *On Contradiction*

NOTES

[1] *Shan Hai Ching (Book of Mountains and Seas)* was written in the era of the Warring States (403-221 B.C.). In one of its fables Kua Fu, a superman, pursued and overtook the sun. But he died of thirst, whereupon his staff was transformed into the forest of Teng.

[2] Yi is one of the legendary heroes of ancient China, famous for his archery. According to a legend in *Huai Nan Tzu*, compiled in the 2nd century B.C., there were ten suns in the sky in the days of Emperor Yao. To put an end to the damage to vegetation caused by these scorching suns, Emperor Yao ordered Yi to shoot them down. In another legend recorded by Wang Yi (2nd century A.D.), the archer is said to have shot down nine of the ten suns.

[3] *Hsi Yu Chi (Pilgrimage to the West)* is a 16th century novel, the hero of which is the monkey god Sun Wu-kung. He could miraculously change at will into seventy-two different shapes, such as a bird, a tree and a stone.

[4] The *Strange Tales of Liao Chai*, written by Pu Sung-ling in the 17th century, is a well-known collection of 431 tales, mostly about ghosts and fox spirits.

[5] Karl Marx, "Introduction to the Critique of Political Economy", *A Contribution to the Critique of Political Economy*, Eng. ed., Chicago, 1904, pp. 310-11.

STUDY

October 1938

Generally speaking, all Communist Party members who can do so should study the theory of Marx, Engels, Lenin and Stalin, study our national history and study current movements and trends; moreover, they should help to educate members with less schooling. The cadres in particular should study these subjects carefully, while members of the Central Committee and senior cadres should give them even more attention. No political party can possibly lead a great revolutionary movement to victory unless it possesses revolutionary theory and a knowledge of history and has a profound grasp of the practical movement.

The theory of Marx, Engels, Lenin and Stalin is universally applicable. We should regard it not as a dogma, but as a guide to action. Studying it is not merely a matter of learning terms and phrases but of learning Marxism-Leninism as the science of revolution. It is not just a matter of understanding the general laws derived by Marx, Engels, Lenin and Stalin from their extensive study of real life and revolutionary experience, but of studying their standpoint and method in examining and solving problems. Our Party's mastery of Marxism-Leninism is now rather better than it used to be, but is still far from being extensive or deep. Ours is the task of leading a great nation of several hundred million in a great and unprecedented struggle. For us, therefore, the spreading and deepening of the study of Marxism-Leninism present a big problem demanding an early solution which is possible only through concentrated effort. Following on this plenary session of the Central Committee, I hope to see an all-Party emulation in study which will show who has really learned something, and who has learned more and learned better. So far as shouldering the main responsibility of leadership is concerned, our Party's fighting capacity will be much greater and our task of defeating Japanese imperialism will be more quickly accomplished if there are one or two hundred comrades with a grasp of Marxism-Leninism which is systematic and not fragmentary, genuine and not hollow.

Another of our tasks is to study our historical heritage and use the Marxist method to sum it up critically. Our national history goes back several thousand years and has its own characteristics and innumerable treasures. But in these matters we are mere schoolboys. Contemporary China has grown out of the China of the past; we are Marxist in our historical approach and must not lop off our history. We should sum up our history from Confucius to Sun Yat-sen and take over this valuable legacy. This is important for guiding the great movement of today. Being Marxists, Communists are internationalists, but we can put Marxism into practice only when it is integrated with the specific characteristics of our country and acquires a definite national form. The great strength of Marxism-Leninism lies precisely in its integration with the concrete revolutionary practice of all countries. For the Chinese Communist Party, it is a matter of learning to apply the theory of Marxism-Leninism to the specific circumstances of China. For the Chinese Communists who are part of the great Chinese nation, flesh of its flesh and blood of its blood, any talk about Marxism in isolation from China's characteristics is merely Marxism in the abstract, Marxism in a vacuum. Hence to apply Marxism concretely in China so that its every manifestation has an indubitably Chinese character, *i.e.*, to apply Marxism in the light of China's specific characteristics, becomes a problem which it is urgent for the whole Party to understand and solve. Foreign stereotypes[1] must be abolished, there must be less singing of empty, abstract tunes, and dogmatism must be laid to rest; they must be replaced by the fresh, lively Chinese style and spirit which the common people of China love. To separate internationalist content from national form is the practice of those who do not understand the first thing about internationalism. We, on the contrary, must link the two closely. In this matter there are serious errors in our ranks which should be conscientiously overcome.

What are the characteristics of the present movement? What are its laws? How is it to be directed? These are all practical questions. To this day we do not yet understand everything about Japanese imperialism, or about China. The movement is developing, new things have yet to emerge, and they are emerging in an endless stream. To study this movement in its entirety and in its development is a great task claiming our constant attention. Whoever refuses to study these problems seriously and carefully is no Marxist.

Complacency is the enemy of study. We cannot really learn anything until we rid ourselves of complacency. Our attitude towards ourselves should be "to be insatiable in learning" and towards others "to be tireless in teaching".

From *The Role of the Chinese Communist Party in the National War*

NOTES

[1] Stereotyped writing, or the "eight-legged essay", was the special form of essay prescribed in the imperial examinations under China's feudal dynasties from the 15th to the 19th centuries; it juggled with words, concentrated only on form and was devoid of content. Every paragraph was written to a rigid pattern and even the number of words was prescribed; the writer spun out the essay by ringing the changes on the words of the theme. The foreign stereotype was developed after the May 4th Movement in 1919 by certain shallow bourgeois and petty-bourgeois intellectuals whose writings resembled the "eight-legged essay", containing nothing but cliches. The foreign stereotype which they spread persisted among revolutionary cultural workers for a long time.

THE MAY 4TH MOVEMENT

May 1939

The May 4th Movement twenty years ago marked a new stage in China's bourgeois-democratic revolution against imperialism and feudalism. The cultural reform movement which grew out of the May 4th Movement was only one of the manifestations of this revolution. With the growth and development of new social forces in that period, a powerful camp made its appearance in the bourgeois-democratic revolution, a camp consisting of the working class, the student masses and the new national bourgeoisie. Around the time of the May 4th Movement, hundreds of thousands of students courageously took their place in the van. In these respects the May 4th Movement went a step beyond the Revolution of 1911.

If we trace China's bourgeois-democratic revolution back to its formative period, we see that it has passed through a number of stages in its development: the Opium War,[1] the War of the Taiping Heavenly Kingdom,[2] the Sino-Japanese War of 1894,[3] the Reform Movement of 1898,[4] the Yi Ho Tuan Movement,[5] the Revolution of 1911,[6] the May 4th Movement, the Northern Expedition,[7] and the War of the Agrarian Revolution.[8] The present War of Resistance Against

---

Comrade Mao Tse-tung wrote this article for newspapers in Yenan to commemorate the twentieth anniversary of the May 4th Movement.

Japan is yet another stage, and is the greatest, most vigorous and most dynamic stage of all. The bourgeois-democratic revolution can be considered accomplished only when the forces of foreign imperialism and domestic feudalism have basically been overthrown and an independent democratic state has been established. From the Opium War onwards each stage in the development of the revolution has had its own distinguishing characteristics. But the most important feature differentiating them is whether they came before or after the emergence of the Communist Party. However, taken as a whole, all the stages bear the character of a bourgeois-democratic revolution. The aim of this democratic revolution is to establish a social system hitherto unknown in Chinese history, namely, a democratic social system having a feudal society (during the last hundred years a semi-colonial and semi-feudal society) as its precursor and a socialist society as its successor. If anyone asks why a Communist should strive to bring into being first a bourgeois-democratic society and then a socialist society, our answer is: we are following the inevitable course of history.

China's democratic revolution depends on definite social forces for its accomplishment. These social forces are the working class, the peasantry, the intelligentsia and the progressive section of the bourgeoisie, that is, the revolutionary workers, peasants, soldiers, students and intellectuals, and businessmen, with the workers and peasants as the basic revolutionary forces and the workers as the class which leads the revolution. It is impossible to accomplish the anti-imperialist and anti-feudal democratic revolution without these basic revolutionary forces and without the leadership of the working class. Today, the principal enemies of the revolution are the Japanese imperialists and the Chinese traitors, and the fundamental policy in the revolution is the policy of the Anti-Japanese National United Front, consisting of all workers, peasants, soldiers, students and intellectuals, and businessmen who are against Japanese aggression. Final victory in the War of Resistance will be won when this united front is greatly consolidated and developed.

In the Chinese democratic revolutionary movement, it was the intellectuals who were the first to awaken. This was clearly demonstrated both in the Revolution of 1911 and in the May 4th Movement, and in the days of the May 4th Movement the intellectuals were more numerous and more politically conscious than in the days of the Revolution of 1911. But the intellectuals will accomplish nothing if they fail to integrate themselves with the workers and peasants. In the final analysis, the dividing line between revolutionary intellectuals and non-revolutionary or counter-revolutionary intellectuals is whether or not they are willing to integrate themselves with the workers and peasants and actually do so. Ultimately it is this alone, and not professions of faith in the Three People's Principles or in Marxism, that distinguishes one from the other. A true revolutionary must be one who is willing to integrate himself with the workers and peasants and actually does so.

It is now twenty years since the May 4th Movement and almost two years since the outbreak of the anti-Japanese war. The young people and the cultural circles of the whole country bear a heavy responsibility in the democratic revolution and the War of Resistance. I hope they will understand the character and the motive forces of the Chinese revolution, make their work serve the workers and peasants, go into their midst and become propagandists and organizers among them.

Victory will be ours when the entire people arises against Japan. Young people of the whole country, bestir yourselves!

NOTES

[1] For many decades, beginning with the end of the 18th century, Britain exported an increasing quantity of opium to China. This traffic not only subjected the Chinese people to drugging but also plundered China of her silver. It aroused fierce opposition in China. In 1840, under the pretext of safeguarding its trade with China, Britain launched armed aggression against her. The Chinese troops led by Lin Tse-hsu put up resistance, and the people in Canton spontaneously organized the "Quell-the-British Corps", which dealt serious blows to the British forces of aggression. In 1842, however, the corrupt Ching regime signed the Treaty of Nanking with the British aggressor. This treaty provided for the payment of indemnities and the cession of Hongkong to Britain, and stipulated that Shanghai, Foochow, Amoy, Ningpo and Canton were to be opened to British trade and that tariff rates for British goods imported into China were to be jointly fixed by China and Britain.

[2] The War of the Taiping Heavenly Kingdom was the mid-19th century revolutionary peasant war against the feudal rule and national oppression of the Ching Dynasty. In January 1851 Hung Hsiu-chuan, Yang Hsiu-ching and other leaders launched an uprising in Chintien Village in Kueiping County, Kwangsi Province, and proclaimed the founding of the Taiping Heavenly Kingdom. Proceeding northward from Kwangsi, their peasant army attacked and occupied Hunan and Hupeh in 1852. In 1853 it marched through Kiangsi and Anhwei and captured Nanking. A section of the forces then continued the drive north and pushed on to the vicinity of Tientsin. However, the Taiping army failed to build stable base areas in the places it occupied; moreover, after establishing its capital in Nanking, its leading group committed many political and military errors. Therefore it was unable to withstand the combined onslaughts of the counter-revolutionary forces of the Ching government and the British, U.S. and French aggressors, and was finally defeated in 1864.

[3] The Sino-Japanese War of 1894-95 was started by Japanese imperialism for the purpose of invading Korea and China. Many Chinese

soldiers and some patriotic generals put up a heroic fight. But China suffered defeat because of the corruption of the Ching government and its failure to prepare resistance. In 1895 the Ching government concluded the shameful Treaty of Shimonoseki with Japan.

[4] The Reform Movement of 1898, whose leading spirits were Kang Yu-wei, Liang Chi-chao and Tan Szu-tung, represented the interests of the liberal bourgeoisie and the enlightened landlords. The movement was favoured and supported by Emperor Kuang Hsu, but had no mass basis. Yuan Shih-kai, who had an army behind him, betrayed the reformers to Empress Dowager Tzu Hsi, the leader of the die-hards, who seized power again and had Emperor Kuang Hsu imprisoned and Tan Szu-tung and five others beheaded. Thus the movement ended in tragic defeat.

[5] The Yi Ho Tuan Movement was the anti-imperialist armed struggle which took place in northern China in 1900. The broad masses of peasants, handicraftsmen and other people took part in this movement. Getting in touch with one another through religious and other channels, they organized themselves on the basis of secret societies and waged a heroic struggle against the joint forces of aggression of the eight imperialist powers — the United States, Britain, Japan, Germany, Russia, France, Italy and Austria. The movement was put down with indescribable savagery after the joint forces of aggression occupied Tientsin and Peking.

[6] The Revolution of 1911 was the bourgeois revolution which overthrew the autocratic regime of the Ching Dynasty. On October 10 of that year, a section of the Ching Dynasty's New Army who were under revolutionary influence staged an uprising in Wuchang, Hupeh Province. The existing bourgeois and petty-bourgeois revolutionary societies and the broad masses of the workers, peasants and soldiers responded enthusiastically, and very soon the rule of the Ching Dynasty crumbled. In January 1912, the Provisional Government of the Republic of China was set up in Nanking, with Sun Yat-sen as the Provisional President. Thus China's feudal monarchic system which had lasted for more than two thousand years was brought to an end. The idea of a democratic republic had entered deep in the hearts of the people. But the bourgeoisie which led the revolution was strongly conciliationist in nature. It did not mobilize the peasant masses on an extensive scale to crush the feudal rule of the landlord class in the countryside, but instead handed state power over to the Northern warlord Yuan Shih-kai under imperialist and feudal pressure. As a result, the revolution ended in defeat.

[7] The Northern Expedition was the punitive war against the Northern warlords launched by the revolutionary army which marched north from Kwangtung Province in May-July 1926. The Northern Expeditionary Army, with the Communist Party of China taking part in its leadership and under the Party's influence (the political work in the army was at that time mostly under the charge of Communist Party members), gained the warm support of the broad masses of workers and peasants. In the second half of 1926 and the first half of 1927 it occupied most of the provinces along the Yangtse and Yellow Rivers and defeated the Northern warlords. In April 1927 this revolutionary war failed as a result of betrayal by the reactionary clique under Chiang Kai-shek within the revolutionary army.

[8] The War of the Agrarian Revolution was the revolutionary struggle of the Chinese people waged under the leadership of the Communist Party from 1927 to 1937, and its main content consisted of the establishment and development of Red political power, the spread of the agrarian revolution and armed resistance to the rule of Kuomintang reaction. This revolutionary war is also known as the Second Revolutionary Civil War.

THE CULTURE OF NEW DEMOCRACY

January 1940

THE CULTURE OF NEW DEMOCRACY

In the foregoing we have explained the historical characteristics of Chinese politics in the new period and the question
of the new-democratic republic. We can now proceed to the
question of culture.

A given culture is the ideological reflection of the politics
and economics of a given society. There is in China an imperialist culture which is a reflection of imperialist rule,
or partial rule, in the political and economic fields. This
culture is fostered not only by the cultural organizations run
directly by the imperialists in China but by a number of Chinese who have lost all sense of shame. Into this category
falls all culture embodying a slave ideology. China also has
a semi-feudal culture which reflects her semi-feudal politics
and economy, and whose exponents include all those who
advocate the worship of Confucius, the study of the Confucian canon, the old ethical code and the old ideas in opposition to the new culture and new ideas. Imperialist culture and
semi-feudal culture are devoted brothers and have formed
a reactionary cultural alliance against China's new culture.
This kind of reactionary culture serves the imperialists and
the feudal class and must be swept away. Unless it is swept

away, no new culture of any kind can be built up. There is no construction without destruction, no flowing without damming and no motion without rest; the two are locked in a life-and-death struggle.

As for the new culture, it is the ideological reflection of the new politics and the new economy which it sets out to serve.

As we have already stated in Section 3, Chinese society has gradually changed in character since the emergence of a capitalist economy in China; it is no longer an entirely feudal but a semi-feudal society, although the feudal economy still predominates. Compared with the feudal economy, this capitalist economy is a new one. The political forces of the bourgeoisie, the petty bourgeoisie and the proletariat are the new political forces which have emerged and grown simultaneously with this new capitalist economy. And the new culture reflects these new economic and political forces in the field of ideology and serves them. Without the capitalist economy, without the bourgeoisie, the petty bourgeoisie and the proletariat, and without the political forces of these classes, the new ideology or new culture could not have emerged.

These new political, economic and cultural forces are all revolutionary forces which are opposed to the old politics, the old economy and the old culture. The old is composed of two parts, one being China's own semi-feudal politics, economy and culture, and the other the politics, economy and culture of imperialism, with the latter heading the alliance. Both are bad and should be completely destroyed. The struggle between the new and the old in Chinese society is a struggle between the new forces of the people (the various revolutionary classes) and the old forces of imperialism and the feudal class. It is a struggle between revolution and counter-revolution. This struggle has lasted a full hundred years if dated from the Opium War, and nearly thirty years if dated from the Revolution of 1911.

But as already indicated, revolutions too can be classified into old and new, and what is new in one historical period becomes old in another. The century of China's bourgeois-democratic revolution can be divided into two main stages, a first stage of eighty years and a second of twenty years. Each has its basic historical characteristics: China's bourgeois-democratic revolution in the first eighty years belongs to the old category, while in the last twenty years, owing to the change in the international and domestic political situation, it belongs to the new category. Old democracy is the characteristic of the first eighty years. New Democracy is the characteristic of the last twenty. This distinction holds good in culture as well as in politics.

How does it manifest itself in the field of culture? We shall explain this next.

THE HISTORICAL CHARACTERISTICS OF CHINA'S CULTURAL REVOLUTION

On the cultural or ideological front, the two periods preceding and following the May 4th Movement form two distinct historical periods.

Before the May 4th Movement, the struggle on China's cultural front was one between the new culture of the bourgeoisie and the old culture of the feudal class. The struggles between the modern school system and the imperial examination system,[1] between the new learning and the old learning, and between Western learning and Chinese learning, were all of this nature. The so-called modern schools or new learning or Western learning of that time concentrated mainly (we say mainly, because in part pernicious vestiges of Chinese feudalism still remained) on the natural sciences and bourgeois social and political theories, which were needed by the representatives of the bourgeoisie. At the time, the ideology of the new learning played a revolutionary role in fighting the Chinese feudal ideology, and it served the bourgeois-democratic revolution of the old period. However, because the Chinese bourgeoisie lacked strength and the world had already entered the era of imperialism, this bourgeois ideology was only able to last out a few rounds and was beaten back by the reactionary alliance of the enslaving ideology of foreign imperialism and the "back to the ancients" ideology of Chinese feudalism; as soon as this reactionary ideological alliance started a minor counter-offensive, the so-called new learning lowered its banners, muffled its drums and beat a retreat, retaining its outer form but losing its soul. The old bourgeois-democratic culture became enervated and decayed in the era of imperialism, and its failure was inevitable.

But since the May 4th Movement things have been different. A brand-new cultural force came into being in China, that is, the communist culture and ideology guided by the Chinese Communists, or the communist world outlook and theory of social revolution. The May 4th Movement occurred in 1919, and in 1921 came the founding of the Chinese Communist Party and the real beginning of China's labour movement — all in the wake of the First World War and the October Revolution, *i.e.*, at a time when the national problem and the colonial revolutionary movements of the world underwent a change, and the connection between the Chinese revolution and the world revolution became quite obvious. The new political force of the proletariat and the Communist

Party entered the Chinese political arena, and as a result, the new cultural force, in new uniform and with new weapons, mustering all possible allies and deploying its ranks in battle array, launched heroic attacks on imperialist culture and feudal culture. This new force has made great strides in the domain of the social sciences and of the arts and letters, whether of philosophy, economics, political science, military science, history, literature or art (including the theatre, the cinema, music, sculpture and painting). For the last twenty years, wherever this new cultural force has directed its attack, a great revolution has taken place both in ideological content and in form (for example, in the written language). Its influence has been so great and its impact so powerful that it is invincible wherever it goes. The numbers it has rallied behind it have no parallel in Chinese history. Lu Hsun was the greatest and the most courageous standard-bearer of this new cultural force. The chief commander of China's cultural revolution, he was not only a great man of letters but a great thinker and revolutionary. Lu Hsun was a man of unyielding integrity, free from all sycophancy or obsequiousness; this quality is invaluable among colonial and semi-colonial peoples. Representing the great majority of the nation, Lu Hsun breached and stormed the enemy citadel; on the cultural front he was the bravest and most correct, the firmest, the most loyal and the most ardent national hero, a hero without parallel in our history. The road he took was the very road of China's new national culture.

Prior to the May 4th Movement, China's new culture was a culture of the old-democratic kind and part of the capitalist cultural revolution of the world bourgeoisie. Since the May 4th Movement, it has become new-democratic and part of the socialist cultural revolution of the world proletariat.

Prior to the May 4th Movement, China's new cultural movement, her cultural revolution, was led by the bourgeoisie, which still had a leading role to play. After the May 4th Movement, its culture and ideology became even more backward than its politics and were incapable of playing any leading role; at most, they could serve to a certain extent as an ally during revolutionary periods, while inevitably the responsibility for leading the alliance rested on proletarian culture and ideology. This is an undeniable fact.

The new-democratic culture is the anti-imperialist and anti-feudal culture of the broad masses; today it is the culture of the anti-Japanese united front. This culture can be led only by the culture and ideology of the proletariat, by the ideology of communism, and not by the culture and ideology of any other class. In a word, new-democratic culture is the proletarian-led, anti-imperialist and anti-feudal culture of the broad masses.

THE FOUR PERIODS

A cultural revolution is the ideological reflection of the political and economic revolution and is in their service. In China there is a united front in the cultural as in the political revolution.

The history of the united front in the cultural revolution during the last twenty years can be divided into four periods. The first covers the two years from 1919 to 1921, the second the six years from 1921 to 1927, the third the ten years from 1927 to 1937, and the fourth the three years from 1937 to the present.

The first period extended from the May 4th Movement of 1919 to the founding of the Chinese Communist Party in 1921. The May 4th Movement was its chief landmark.

The May 4th Movement was an anti-imperialist as well as an anti-feudal movement. Its outstanding historical significance is to be seen in a feature which was absent from the Revolution of 1911, namely, its thorough and uncompromising opposition to imperialism as well as to feudalism. The May 4th Movement possessed this quality because capitalism had developed a step further in China and because new hopes had arisen for the liberation of the Chinese nation as China's revolutionary intellectuals saw the collapse of three great imperialist powers, Russia, Germany and Austria-Hungary, and the weakening of two others, Britain and France, while the Russian proletariat had established a socialist state and the German, Hungarian and Italian proletariat had risen in revolution. The May 4th Movement came into being at the call of the world revolution, of the Russian Revolution and of Lenin. It was part of the world proletarian revolution of the time. Although the Communist Party had not yet come into existence, there were already large numbers of intellectuals who approved of the Russian Revolution and had the rudiments of communist ideology. In the beginning the May 4th Movement was the revolutionary movement of a united front of three sections of people — communist intellectuals, revolutionary petty-bourgeois intellectuals and bourgeois intellectuals (the last forming the right wing of the movement). Its shortcoming was that it was confined to the intellectuals and that the workers and peasants did not join in. But as soon as it developed into the June 3rd Movement, not only the intellectuals but the mass of the proletariat, the petty bourgeoisie and the bourgeoisie joined in, and it became a

64

nation-wide revolutionary movement. The cultural revolution ushered in by the May 4th Movement was uncompromising in its opposition to feudal culture; there had never been such a great and thoroughgoing cultural revolution since the dawn of Chinese history. Raising aloft the two great banners of the day, "Down with the old ethics and up with the new!" and "Down with the old literature and up with the new!", the cultural revolution had great achievements to its credit. At that time it was not yet possible for this cultural movement to become widely diffused among the workers and peasants. The slogan of "Literature for the common people" was advanced, but in fact the "common people" then could only refer to the petty-bourgeois and bourgeois intellectuals in the cities, that is, the urban intelligentsia. Both in ideology and in the matter of cadres, the May 4th Movement paved the way for the founding of the Chinese Communist Party in 1921 and for the May 30th Movement in 1925[2] and the Northern Expedition. The bourgeois intellectuals, who constituted the right wing of the May 4th Movement, mostly compromised with the enemy in the second period and went over to the side of reaction.

In the second period, whose landmarks were the founding of the Chinese Communist Party, the May 30th Movement and the Northern Expedition, the united front of the three classes formed in the May 4th Movement was continued and expanded, the peasantry was drawn into it and a political united front of all these classes, the first instance of Kuomintang-Communist co-operation, was established. Dr. Sun Yat-sen was a great man not only because he led the great Revolution of 1911 (although it was only a democratic revolution of the old period), but also because, "adapting himself to the trends of the world and meeting

the needs of the masses", he had the capacity to bring forward the revolutionary Three Great Policies of alliance with
Russia, co-operation with the Communist Party and assistance
to the peasants and workers, give new meaning to the Three
People's Principles[3] and thus institute the new Three People's
Principles with their Three Great Policies. Previously, the
Three People's Principles had exerted little influence on the
educational and academic world or with the youth, because
they had not raised the issues of opposition to imperialism or
to the feudal social system and feudal culture and ideology.
They were the old Three People's Principles which people regarded as the time-serving banner of a group of men bent on
seizing power, in other words, on securing official positions, a
banner used purely for political manoeuvring. Then came
the new Three People's Principles with their Three Great
Policies. The co-operation between the Kuomintang and the
Communist Party and the joint efforts of the revolutionary
members of the two parties spread the new Three People's
Principles all over China, extending to a section of the educational and academic world and the mass of student youth.
This was entirely due to the fact that the original Three
People's Principles had developed into the anti-imperialist,
anti-feudal and new-democratic Three People's Principles
with their Three Great Policies. Without this development
it would have been impossible to disseminate the ideas of
the Three People's Principles.

During this period, the revolutionary Three People's Principles became the political basis of the united front of the
Kuomintang and the Communist Party and of all the revolutionary classes, and since "communism is the good friend of
the Three People's Principles", a united front was formed
between the two of them. In terms of social classes, it was a

66

united front of the proletariat, the peasantry, the urban petty bourgeoisie and the bourgeoisie. Using the Communist *Weekly Guide*, the Kuomintang's *Republican Daily News* of Shanghai and other newspapers in various localities as their bases of operations, the two parties jointly advocated anti-imperialism, jointly combated feudal education based upon the worship of Confucius and upon the study of the Confucian canon and jointly opposed feudal literature and the classical language and promoted the new literature and the vernacular style of writing with an anti-imperialist and anti-feudal content. During the wars in Kwangtung and during the Northern Expedition, they reformed China's armed forces by the inculcation of anti-imperialist and anti-feudal ideas. The slogans, "Down with the corrupt officials" and "Down with the local tyrants and evil gentry", were raised among the peasant millions, and great peasant revolutionary struggles were aroused. Thanks to all this and to the assistance of the Soviet Union, the Northern Expedition was victorious. But no sooner did the big bourgeoisie climb to power than it put an end to this revolution, thus creating an entirely new political situation.

The third period was the new revolutionary period of 1927-37. As a change had taken place within the revolutionary camp towards the end of the second period, with the big bourgeoisie going over to the counter-revolutionary camp of the imperialist and feudal forces and the national bourgeoisie trailing after it, only three of the four classes formerly within the revolutionary camp remained, *i.e.*, the proletariat, the peasantry and the other sections of the petty bourgeoisie (including the revolutionary intellectuals), and consequently the Chinese revolution inevitably entered a new period in which the Chinese Communist Party alone gave leadership to the masses. This period was one of counter-revolutionary campaigns of "encirclement and suppression", on the one hand, and of the deepening of the revolution, on the other. There were two kinds of counter-revolutionary campaigns of "encirclement and suppression", the military and the cultural. The deepening of the revolution was of two kinds; both the agrarian and the cultural revolutions were deepened. At the instigation of the imperialists, the counter-revolutionary forces of the whole country and of the whole world were mobilized for both kinds of campaigns of "encirclement and suppression", which lasted no less than ten years and were unparalleled in their ruthlessness; hundreds of thousands of Communists and young students were slaughtered and millions of workers and peasants suffered cruel persecution. The people responsible for all this apparently had no doubt that communism and the Communist Party could be "exterminated once and for all". However, the outcome was different; both kinds of "encirclement and suppression" campaigns failed miserably. The military campaign resulted in the northern march of the Red Army to resist the Japanese, and the cultural campaign resulted in the outbreak of the December 9th Movement of the revolutionary youth in 1935.[4] And the common result of both was the awakening of the people of the whole country. These were three positive results. The most amazing thing of all was that the Kuomintang's cultural "encirclement and suppression" campaign failed completely in the Kuomintang areas as well, although the Communist Party was in an utterly defenceless position in all the cultural and educational institutions there. Why did this happen? Does it not give food for prolonged and deep thought? It was in the very midst of such campaigns of "encirclement and suppression" that Lu Hsun, who believed in communism, became the giant of China's cultural revolution.

The negative result of the counter-revolutionary campaigns of "encirclement and suppression" was the invasion of our country by Japanese imperialism. This is the chief reason why to this very day the people of the whole country still bitterly detest those ten years of anti-communism.

In the struggles of this period, the revolutionary side firmly upheld the people's anti-imperialist and anti-feudal New Democracy and their new Three People's Principles, while the counter-revolutionary side, under the direction of imperialism, imposed the despotic regime of the coalition of the landlord class and the big bourgeoisie. That despotic regime butchered Dr. Sun Yat-sen's Three Great Policies and his new Three People's Principles both politically and culturally, with catastrophic consequences to the Chinese nation.

The fourth period is that of the present anti-Japanese war. Pursuing its zigzag course, the Chinese revolution has again arrived at a united front of the four classes; but the scope of the united front is now much broader because its upper stratum includes many members of the ruling classes, its middle stratum includes the national bourgeoisie and the petty bourgeoisie, and its lower stratum includes the entire proletariat, so that the various classes and strata of the nation have become members of the alliance resolutely resisting Japanese imperialism. The first stage of this period lasted until the fall of Wuhan. During that stage, there was a lively atmosphere in the country in every field; politically there was a trend towards democracy and culturally there was fairly widespread activity. With the fall of Wuhan the second stage began, during which the political situation has undergone many changes, with one section of the big bourgeoisie capitulating to the enemy and another desiring an early end to the War of Resistance. In the cultural sphere, this situation has been reflected in the reactionary activities of Yeh Ching,[5] Chang Chun-mai and others, and in the suppression of freedom of speech and of the press.

To overcome this crisis, a firm struggle is necessary against all ideas opposed to resistance, unity and progress, and unless these reactionary ideas are crushed, there will be no hope of victory. How will this struggle turn out? This is the big question in the minds of the people of the whole country. Judging by the domestic and international situation, the Chinese people are bound to win, however numerous the obstacles on the path of resistance. The progress achieved during the twenty years since the May 4th Movement exceeds not only that of the preceding eighty years but virtually surpasses that achieved in the thousands of years of Chinese history. Can we not visualize what further progress China will make in another twenty years? The unbridled violence of all the forces of darkness, whether domestic or foreign, has brought disaster to our nation; but this very violence indicates that while the forces of darkness still have some strength left, they are already in their death throes, and that the people are gradually approaching victory. This is true of China, of the whole East and of the entire world.

SOME WRONG IDEAS ABOUT THE NATURE OF CULTURE

Everything new comes from the forge of hard and bitter struggle. This is also true of the new culture which has followed a zigzag course in the past twenty years, during which both the good and the bad were tested and proved in struggle.

The bourgeois die-hards are as hopelessly wrong on the question of culture as on that of political power. They neither understand the historical characteristics of this new period in China, nor recognize the new-democratic culture of the masses. Their starting point is bourgeois despotism, which in culture becomes the cultural despotism of the bourgeoisie. It seems that a section (and I refer only to a section) of educated people from the so-called European-American school[6] who in fact supported the Kuomintang government's "Communist suppression" campaign on the cultural front in the past are now supporting its policy of "restricting" and "corroding" the Communist Party. They do not want the workers and the peasants to hold up their heads politically or culturally. This bourgeois die-hard road of cultural despotism leads nowhere; as in the case of political despotism, the domestic and international pre-conditions are lacking. Therefore this cultural despotism, too, had better be "folded up".

So far as the orientation of our national culture is concerned, communist ideology plays the guiding role, and we should work hard both to disseminate socialism and communism throughout the working class and to educate the peasantry and other sections of the people in socialism properly and step by step. However, our national culture as a whole is not yet socialist.

Because of the leadership of the proletariat, the politics, the economy and the culture of New Democracy all contain an element of socialism, and by no means a mere casual element but one with a decisive role. However, taken as a whole, the political, economic and cultural situation so far is new-democratic and not socialist. For the Chinese revolution in its present stage is not yet a socialist revolution for the overthrow of capitalism but a bourgeois-democratic revolution, its central task being mainly that of combating foreign imperialism and domestic feudalism. In the sphere of national culture, it is wrong to assume that the existing national culture is, or should be, socialist in its entirety. That would amount to confusing the dissemination of communist ideology with the carrying out of an immediate programme of action, and to confusing the application of the communist standpoint and method in investigating problems, undertaking research, handling work and training cadres with the general policy for national education and national culture in the democratic stage of the Chinese revolution. A national culture with a socialist content will necessarily be the reflection of a socialist politics and a socialist economy. There are socialist elements in our politics and our economy, and hence these socialist elements are reflected in our national culture; but taking our society as a whole, we do not have a socialist politics and a socialist economy yet, so that there cannot be a wholly socialist national culture. Since the present Chinese revolution is part of the world proletarian-socialist revolution, the new culture of China today is part of the world proletarian-socialist new culture and is its great ally. While this part contains vital elements of socialist culture, the national culture as a whole joins the stream of the world proletarian-socialist new culture not entirely as a socialist culture, but as the anti-imperialist and anti-feudal new-democratic culture of the broad masses. And since the Chinese revolution today cannot do without proletarian leadership, China's new culture cannot do without the leadership of proletarian culture and ideology, of communist ideology. At the present stage, however, this kind of leadership means leading the masses of the people in an anti-imperialist and anti-feudal political and cultural revolution, and therefore, taken as a whole, the content of China's new national culture is still not socialist but new-democratic.

Beyond all doubt, now is the time to spread communist ideas more widely and put more energy into the study of Marxism-Leninism, or otherwise we shall not only be unable to lead the Chinese revolution forward to the future stage of socialism, but shall also be unable to guide the present democratic revolution to victory. However, we must keep the spreading of communist ideas and propaganda about the communist social system distinct from the practical application of the new-democratic programme of action; we must also keep the communist theory and method of investigating problems, undertaking research, handling work and training cadres distinct from the new-democratic line for national culture as a whole. It is undoubtedly inappropriate to mix the two up.

It can thus be seen that the content of China's new national culture at the present stage is neither the cultural despotism of the bourgeoisie nor the socialism of the proletariat, but the anti-imperialist and anti-feudal New Democracy of the masses, under the leadership of proletarian-socialist culture and ideology.

A NATIONAL, SCIENTIFIC AND MASS CULTURE

New-democratic culture is national. It opposes imperialist oppression and upholds the dignity and independence of the Chinese nation. It belongs to our own nation and bears our own national characteristics. It links up with the socialist and new-democratic cultures of all other nations and they are related in such a way that they can absorb something from each other and help each other to develop, together forming a new world culture; but as a revolutionary national culture it can never link up with any reactionary imperialist culture of whatever nation. To nourish her own culture China needs to assimilate a good deal of foreign progressive culture, not enough of which was done in the past. We should assimilate whatever is useful to us today not only from the present-day socialist and new-democratic cultures but also from the earlier cultures of other nations, for example, from the culture of the various capitalist countries in the Age of Enlightenment. However, we should not gulp any of this foreign material down uncritically, but must treat it as we do our food — first chewing it, then submitting it to the working of the stomach and intestines with their juices and secretions, and separating it into nutriment to be absorbed and waste matter to be discarded — before it can nourish us. To advocate "wholesale westernization"[7] is wrong. China has suffered a great deal from the mechanical absorption of foreign material. Similarly, in applying Marxism to China, Chinese communists must fully and properly integrate the universal truth of Marxism with the concrete practice of the Chinese revolution, or in other words, the universal truth of Marxism must be combined with specific national characteristics and acquire a definite national form if it is to be useful, and in no circumstances can it be applied subjectively as a mere formula. Marxists who make a fetish of formulas are simply playing the fool with Marxism and the Chinese revolution, and there is no room for them in the ranks of the

Chinese revolution. Chinese culture should have its own form, its own national form. National in form and new-democratic in content — such is our new culture today.

New-democratic culture is scientific. Opposed as it is to all feudal and superstitious ideas, it stands for seeking truth from facts, for objective truth and for the unity of theory and practice. On this point, the possibility exists of a united front against imperialism, feudalism and superstition between the scientific thought of the Chinese proletariat and those Chinese bourgeois materialists and natural scientists who are progressive, but in no case is there a possibility of a united front with any reactionary idealism. In the field of political action Communists may form an anti-imperialist and anti-feudal united front with some idealists and even religious people, but we can never approve of their idealism or religious doctrines. A splendid old culture was created during the long period of Chinese feudal society. To study the development of this old culture, to reject its feudal dross and assimilate its democratic essence is a necessary condition for developing our new national culture and increasing our national self-confidence, but we should never swallow anything and everything uncritically. It is imperative to separate the fine old culture of the people which had a more or less democratic and revolutionary character from all the decadence of the old feudal ruling class. China's present new politics and new economy have developed out of her old politics and old economy, and her present new culture, too, has developed out of her old culture; therefore, we must respect our own history and must not lop it off. However, respect for history means giving it its proper place as a science, respecting its dialectical development, and not eulogizing the past at the expense of the present or praising every drop of feudal poison.

As far as the masses and the young students are concerned, the essential thing is to guide them to look forward and not backward.

New-democratic culture belongs to the broad masses and is therefore democratic. It should serve the toiling masses of workers and peasants who make up more than 90 per cent of the nation's population and should gradually become their very own. There is a difference of degree, as well as a close link, between the knowledge imparted to the revolutionary cadres and the knowledge imparted to the revolutionary masses, between the raising of cultural standards and popularization. Revolutionary culture is a powerful revolutionary weapon for the broad masses of the people. It prepares the ground ideologically before the revolution comes and is an important, indeed essential, fighting front in the general revolutionary front during the revolution. People engaged in revolutionary cultural work are the commanders at various levels on this cultural front. "Without revolutionary theory there can be no revolutionary movement";[8] one can thus see how important the cultural movement is for the practical revolutionary movement. Both the cultural and practical movements must be of the masses. Therefore all progressive cultural workers in the anti-Japanese war must have their own cultural battalions, that is, the broad masses. A revolutionary cultural worker who is not close to the people is a commander without an army, whose fire-power cannot bring the enemy down. To attain this objective, written Chinese must be reformed, given the requisite conditions, and our spoken language brought closer to that of the people, for the people, it must be stressed, are the inexhaustible source of our revolutionary culture.

A national, scientific and mass culture — such is the anti-imperialist and anti-feudal culture of the people, the culture of New Democracy, the new culture of the Chinese nation.

Combine the politics, the economy and the culture of New Democracy, and you have the new-democratic republic, the Republic of China both in name and in reality, the new China we want to create.

Behold, New China is within sight. Let us all hail her!

Her masts have already risen above the horizon. Let us all cheer in welcome!

Raise both your hands. New China is ours!

From *On New Democracy*

NOTES

[1] The modern school system was the educational system modelled on that of capitalist countries in Europe and America. The imperial examination system was the old examination system in feudal China. Towards the end of the 19th century, enlightened Chinese intellectuals urged the abolition of the old competitive examination system and the establishment of modern schools.

[2] The May 30th Movement was the nation-wide anti-imperialist movement in protest against the massacre of the Chinese people by the British police in Shanghai on May 30, 1925. Earlier that month, major strikes had broken out in Japanese-owned textile mills in Tsingtao and Shanghai, which the Japanese imperialists and the Northern warlords who were their running dogs proceeded to suppress. On May 15 the Japanese textile mill-owners in Shanghai shot and killed the worker Ku Cheng-hung and wounded a dozen others. On May 28 eight workers were slaughtered by the reactionary government in Tsingtao. On May 30 more than two thousand students in Shanghai agitated in the foreign concessions in support of the workers and for the recovery of the foreign concessions. They rallied more than ten thousand people before the

British police headquarters, shouting such slogans as "Down with imperialism!" and "People of China, unite!" The British imperialist police opened fire, killing and wounding many students. This became known as the May 30th Massacre. It immediately aroused country-wide indignation, and demonstrations and strikes of workers, students and shopkeepers were held everywhere, forming a tremendous anti-imperialist movement.

[3] The Three People's Principles were the principles and the programme put forward by Sun Yat-sen on the questions of nationalism, democracy and people's livelihood in China's bourgeois-democratic revolution. In the manifesto adopted by the Kuomintang at its First National Congress in 1924 Sun Yat-sen restated the Three People's Principles. Nationalism was interpreted as opposition to imperialism and active support was expressed for the movements of the workers and peasants. Thus the old Three People's Principles were transformed into the new Three People's Principles characterized by the Three Great Policies, that is, alliance with Russia, co-operation with the Communist Party, and assistance to the peasants and workers. The new Three People's Principles provided the political basis for the co-operation between the Communist Party of China and the Kuomintang during the First Revolutionary Civil War period.

[4] The year 1935 witnessed a new upsurge in the popular patriotic movement throughout the country. Students in Peking, under the leadership of the Communist Party of China, held a patriotic demonstration on December 9, putting forward such slogans as "Stop the civil war and unite to resist foreign aggression" and "Down with Japanese imperialism". This movement broke through the long reign of terror imposed by the Kuomintang government in league with the Japanese invaders and very quickly won the people's support throughout the country. It is known as the "December 9th Movement". The outcome was that new changes manifested themselves in the relations among the various classes in the country, and the Anti-Japanese National United Front proposed by the Communist Party of China became the openly advocated policy of all patriotic people. The Chiang Kai-shek government with its traitorous policy became very isolated.

[5] Yeh Ching was a renegade Communist who became a hired hack in the Kuomintang secret service.

[6] The spokesman of the so-called European-American school was the counter-revolutionary Hu Shih.

7 Wholesale westernization was the view held by a number of westernized Chinese bourgeois intellectuals who unconditionally praised the outmoded individualist bourgeois culture of the West and advocated the servile imitation of capitalist Europe and America.

8 V. I. Lenin, "What Is to Be Done?", *Collected Works*, Eng. ed., FLPH, Moscow, 1961, Vol. V, p. 369.

REFORM OUR STUDY

May 1941

I propose that we should reform the method and the system of study throughout the Party. The reasons are as follows:

The twenty years of the Communist Party of China have been twenty years in which the universal truth of Marxism-Leninism has become more and more integrated with the concrete practice of the Chinese revolution. If we recall how superficial and meagre our understanding of Marxism-Leninism and of the Chinese revolution was during our Party's infancy, we can see how much deeper and richer it is now. For a hundred years, the finest sons and daughters of the disaster-ridden Chinese nation fought and sacrificed their lives, one stepping into the breach as another fell, in quest of the truth that would save the country and the people. This moves us to song and tears. But it was only after World War

---

Comrade Mao Tse-tung made this report to a cadres' meeting in Yenan. The report and the two articles, "Rectify the Party's Style of Work" and "Oppose Stereotyped Party Writing", are Comrade Mao Tse-tung's basic works on the rectification movement. In these he summed up, on the ideological plane, past differences in the Party over the Party line and analysed the petty-bourgeois ideology and style which, masquerading as Marxism-Leninism, were prevalent in the Party, and which chiefly manifested themselves in subjectivist and sectarian tendencies,

I and the October Revolution in Russia that we found Marxism-Leninism, the best of truths, the best of weapons for liberating our nation. And the Communist Party of China has been the initiator, propagandist and organizer in the wielding of this weapon. As soon as it was linked with the concrete practice of the Chinese revolution, the universal truth of Marxism-Leninism gave an entirely new complexion to the Chinese revolution. Since the outbreak of the War of Resistance Against Japan, our Party, basing itself on the universal truth of Marxism-Leninism, has taken a further step in its study of the concrete practice of this war and in its study of China and the world today, and has also made a beginning in the study of Chinese history. These are all very good signs.

II

However, we still have shortcomings, and very big ones too. Unless we correct these shortcomings, we shall not, in my opinion, be able to take another step forward in our work and in our great cause of integrating the universal truth of Marxism-Leninism with the concrete practice of the Chinese revolution.

First, take the study of current conditions. We have achieved some success in our study of present domestic and

---

their form of expression being stereotyped Party writing. Comrade Mao Tse-tung called for a Party-wide movement of Marxist-Leninist education to rectify style of work in accordance with the ideological principles of Marxism-Leninism. His call very quickly led to a great debate between proletarian and petty-bourgeois ideology inside and outside the Party. This consolidated the position of proletarian ideology inside and outside the Party, enabled the broad ranks of cadres to take a great step forward ideologically and the Party to achieve unprecedented unity.

international conditions, but for such a large political party as ours, the material we have collected is fragmentary and our research work unsystematic on each and every aspect of these subjects, whether it be the political, military, economic or cultural aspect. Generally speaking, in the last twenty years we have not done systematic and thorough work in collecting and studying material on these aspects, and we are lacking in a climate of investigation and study of objective reality. To behave like "a blindfolded man catching sparrows", or "a blind man groping for fish", to be crude and careless, to indulge in verbiage, to rest content with a smattering of knowledge — such is the extremely bad style of work that still exists among many comrades in our Party, a style utterly opposed to the fundamental spirit of Marxism-Leninism. Marx, Engels, Lenin and Stalin have taught us that it is necessary to study conditions conscientiously and to proceed from objective reality and not from subjective wishes; but many of our comrades act in direct violation of this truth.

Second, take the study of history. Although a few Party members and sympathizers have undertaken this work, it has not been done in an organized way. Many Party members are still in a fog about Chinese history, whether of the last hundred years or of ancient times. There are many Marxist-Leninist scholars who cannot open their mouths without citing ancient Greece; but as for their own ancestors — sorry, they have been forgotten. There is no climate of serious study either of current conditions or of past history.

Third, take the study of international revolutionary experience, the study of the universal truth of Marxism-Leninism. Many comrades seem to study Marxism-Leninism not to meet the needs of revolutionary practice, but purely for the sake of study. Consequently, though they read, they cannot digest. They can only cite odd quotations from Marx, Engels, Lenin and Stalin in a one-sided manner, but are unable to apply the stand, viewpoint and method of Marx, Engels, Lenin and Stalin to the concrete study of China's present conditions and her history or to the concrete analysis and solution of the problems of the Chinese revolution. Such an attitude towards Marxism-Leninism does a great deal of harm, particularly among cadres of the middle and higher ranks.

The three aspects I have just mentioned, neglect of the study of current conditions, neglect of the study of history and neglect of the application of Marxism-Leninism, all constitute an extremely bad style of work. Its spread has harmed many of our comrades.

There are indeed many comrades in our ranks who have been led astray by this style of work. Unwilling to carry on systematic and thorough investigation and study of the specific conditions inside and outside the country, the province, county or district, they issue orders on no other basis than their scanty knowledge and "It must be so because it seems so to me". Does not this subjectivist style still exist among a great many comrades?

There are some who are proud, instead of ashamed, of knowing nothing or very little of our own history. What is particularly significant is that very few really know the history of the Communist Party of China and the history of China in the hundred years since the Opium War. Hardly anyone has seriously taken up the study of the economic, political, military and cultural history of the last hundred years. Ignorant of their own country, some people can only relate tales of ancient Greece and other foreign lands, and even this knowledge is quite pathetic, consisting of odds and ends from old foreign books.

For several decades, many of the returned students from abroad have suffered from this malady. Coming home from Europe, America or Japan, they can only parrot things foreign. They become gramophones and forget their duty to understand and create new things. This malady has also infected the Communist Party.

Although we are studying Marxism, the way many of our people study it runs directly counter to Marxism. That is to say, they violate the fundamental principle earnestly enjoined on us by Marx, Engels, Lenin and Stalin, the unity of theory and practice. Having violated this principle, they invent an opposite principle of their own, the separation of theory from practice. In the schools and in the education of cadres at work, teachers of philosophy do not guide students to study the logic of the Chinese revolution; teachers of economics do not guide them to study the characteristics of the Chinese economy; teachers of political science do not guide them to study the tactics of the Chinese revolution; teachers of military science do not guide them to study the strategy and tactics adapted to China's special features; and so on and so forth. Consequently, error is disseminated, doing people great harm. A person does not know how to apply in Fuhsien[1] what he has learned in Yenan. Professors of economics cannot explain the relationship between the Border Region currency and the Kuomintang currency,[2] so naturally the students cannot explain it either. Thus a perverse mentality has been created among many students; instead of showing an interest in China's problems and taking the Party's directives seriously, they give all their hearts to the supposedly eternal and immutable dogmas learned from their teachers.

Of course, what I have just said refers to the worst type in our Party, and I am not saying that it is the general case. However, people of this type do exist; what is more, there are quite a few of them and they cause a great deal of harm. This matter should not be treated lightly.

III

In order to explain this idea further, I should like to contrast two opposite attitudes.

First, there is the subjectivist attitude.

With this attitude, a person does not make a systematic and thorough study of the environment, but works by sheer subjective enthusiasm and has a blurred picture of the face of China today. With this attitude, he chops up history, knows only ancient Greece but not China and is in a fog about the China of yesterday and the day before yesterday. With this attitude, a person studies Marxist-Leninist theory in the abstract and without any aim. He goes to Marx, Engels, Lenin and Stalin not to seek the stand, viewpoint and method with which to solve the theoretical and tactical problems of the Chinese revolution but to study theory purely for theory's sake. He does not shoot the arrow at the target but shoots at random. Marx, Engels, Lenin and Stalin have taught us that we should proceed from objective realities and that we should derive laws from them to serve as our guide to action. For this purpose, we should, as Marx has said, appropriate the material in detail and subject it to scientific analysis and synthesis.[3] Many of our people do not act in this way but do the opposite. A good number of them are doing research work but have no interest in studying either the China of today or the China of yesterday and confine their interest to the study of empty "theories" divorced from reality. Many

85

others are doing practical work, but they too pay no attention to the study of objective conditions, often rely on sheer enthusiasm and substitute their personal feelings for policy. Both kinds of people, relying on the subjective, ignore the existence of objective realities. When making speeches, they indulge in a long string of headings, A, B, C, D, 1, 2, 3, 4, and when writing articles, they turn out a lot of verbiage. They have no intention of seeking truth from facts, but only a desire to curry favour by claptrap. They are flashy without substance, brittle without solidity. They are always right, they are the Number One authority under Heaven, "imperial envoys" who rush everywhere. Such is the style of work of some comrades in our ranks. To govern one's own conduct by this style is to harm oneself, to teach it to others is to harm others, and to use it to direct the revolution is to harm the revolution. To sum up, this subjectivist method which is contrary to science and Marxism-Leninism is a formidable enemy of the Communist Party, the working class, the people and the nation; it is a manifestation of impurity in Party spirit. A formidable enemy stands before us, and we must overthrow him. Only when subjectivism is overthrown can the truth of Marxism-Leninism prevail, can Party spirit be strengthened, can the revolution be victorious. We must assert that the absence of a scientific attitude, that is, the absence of the Marxist-Leninist approach of uniting theory and practice, means that Party spirit is either absent or deficient.

There is a couplet which portrays this type of person. It runs:

> *The reed growing on the wall — top-heavy,*
> *thin-stemmed and shallow of root;*

86

The bamboo shoot in the hills — sharp-tongued,
thick-skinned and hollow inside.

Is this not an apt description of those who do not have a scientific attitude, who can only recite words and phrases from the works of Marx, Engels, Lenin and Stalin and who enjoy a reputation unwarranted by any real learning? If anyone really wishes to cure himself of his malady, I advise him to commit this couplet to memory or to show still more courage and paste it on the wall of his room. Marxism-Leninism is a science, and science means honest, solid knowledge; there is no room for playing tricks. Let us, then, be honest.

Secondly, there is the Marxist-Leninist attitude.

With this attitude, a person applies the theory and method of Marxism-Leninism to the systematic and thorough investigation and study of the environment. He does not work by enthusiasm alone but, as Stalin says, combines revolutionary sweep with practicalness.[4] With this attitude he will not chop up history. It is not enough for him to know ancient Greece, he must know China; he must know the revolutionary history not only of foreign countries but also of China, not only the China of today but also the China of yesterday and of the day before yesterday. With this attitude, one studies the theory of Marxism-Leninism with a purpose, that is, to integrate Marxist-Leninist theory with the actual movement of the Chinese revolution and to seek from this theory the stand, viewpoint and method with which to solve the theoretical and tactical problems of the Chinese revolution. Such an attitude is one of shooting the arrow at the target. The "target" is the Chinese revolution, the "arrow" is Marxism-Leninism. We Chinese Communists have been seeking this

87

arrow because we want to hit the target of the Chinese revolution and of the revolution of the East. To take such an attitude is to seek truth from facts. "Facts" are all the things that exist objectively, "truth" means their internal relations, that is, the laws governing them, and "to seek" means to study. We should proceed from the actual conditions inside and outside the country, the province, county or district, and derive from them, as our guide to action, laws which are inherent in them and not imaginary, that is, we should find the internal relations of the events occurring around us. And in order to do that we must rely not on subjective imagination, not on momentary enthusiasm, not on lifeless books, but on facts that exist objectively; we must appropriate the material in detail and, guided by the general principles of Marxism-Leninism, draw correct conclusions from it. Such conclusions are not mere lists of phenomena in A, B, C, D order or writings full of platitudes, but are scientific conclusions. Such an attitude is one of seeking truth from facts and not of currying favour by claptrap. It is the manifestation of Party spirit, the Marxist-Leninist style of uniting theory and practice. It is the attitude every Communist Party member should have at the very least. He who adopts this attitude will be neither "top-heavy, thin-stemmed and shallow of root" nor "sharp-tongued, thick-skinned and hollow inside".

IV

In accordance with the above views, I would like to make the following proposals:

1. We should place before the whole Party the task of making a systematic and thorough study of the situation

around us. On the basis of the theory and method of Marxism-Leninism, we should make a detailed investigation and study of developments in the economic, financial, political, military, cultural and party activities of our enemies, our friends and ourselves, and then draw the proper and necessary conclusions. To this end, we should direct our comrades' attention to the investigation and study of these practical matters. We should get our comrades to understand that the twofold basic task of the leading bodies of the Communist Party is to know conditions and to master policy; the former means knowing the world and the latter changing the world. We should get our comrades to understand that without investigation there is no right to speak, and that bombastic twaddle and a mere list of phenomena in 1, 2, 3, 4 order are of no use. Take propaganda work, for instance; if we do not know the situation with regard to the propaganda of our enemies, our friends and ourselves, we shall be unable to decide on a correct propaganda policy. In the work of any department, it is necessary to know the situation first and only then can the work be well handled. The fundamental link in changing the Party's style of work is to carry out plans for investigation and study throughout the Party.

2. As for China's history in the last hundred years, we should assemble qualified persons to study it, in co-operation and with a proper division of labour, and so overcome the present disorganized state of affairs. First it is necessary to make analytical studies in the several fields of economic history, political history, military history and cultural history, and only then will it be possible to make synthetical studies.

3. As for education for cadres whether at work or in schools for cadres, a policy should be established of focusing

such education on the study of the practical problems of the Chinese revolution and using the basic principles of Marxism-Leninism as the guide, and the method of studying Marxism-Leninism statically and in isolation should be discarded. Moreover, in studying Marxism-Leninism, we should use the *History of the Communist Party of the Soviet Union (Bolsheviks), Short Course* as the principal material. It is the best synthesis and summing-up of the world communist movement of the past hundred years, a model of the integration of theory and practice, and so far the only comprehensive model in the whole world. When we see how Lenin and Stalin integrated the universal truth of Marxism with the concrete practice of the Soviet revolution and thereby developed Marxism, we shall know how we should work in China.

We have made many detours. But error is often the precursor of what is correct. I am confident that in the context of the Chinese revolution and the world revolution, which is so intensely alive and so richly varied, this reform of our study will certainly yield good results.

NOTES

[1] Fuhsien County is about seventy kilometres south of Yenan.

[2] The Border Region currency consisted of the currency notes issued by the Bank of the Shensi-Kansu-Ningsia Border Region Government. The Kuomintang currency was the paper currency issued by the four big Kuomintang bureaucrat-capitalist banks from 1935 onwards with British and U.S. imperialist support. Comrade Mao Tse-tung was referring to the fluctuations in the rates of exchange between these two currencies.

[3] See Karl Marx, "Afterword to the Second German Edition" of *Capital* in which he wrote: "The latter [the method of inquiry] has to

appropriate the material in detail, to analyse its different forms of development, to trace out their inner connexion. Only after this work is done, can the actual movement be adequately described." (*Capital,* Eng. ed., FLPH, Moscow, 1954, Vol. I, p. 19.)

[4] See J. V. Stalin, "The Foundations of Leninism", *Problems of Leninism,* Russ. ed., Moscow, 1952, p. 80.

OPPOSE STEREOTYPED PARTY WRITING

February 8, 1942

Comrade Kai-feng has just stated the purpose of today's meeting. I now want to discuss the ways subjectivism and sectarianism use stereotyped Party writing (or the Party "eight-legged essay") as their instrument of propaganda or form of expression. We are fighting against subjectivism and sectarianism, but they will still have a hiding-place to lurk in if at the same time we do not get rid of stereotyped Party writing. If we destroy that too, we shall "checkmate" subjectivism and sectarianism and make both these monsters show themselves in their true colours, and then we shall easily be able to annihilate them, like "rats running across the street with everyone yelling: Kill them! Kill them!"

It does not matter much if a person produces stereotyped Party writings only for himself to read. If he passes them on to someone else, the number of readers is doubled, and already no small harm is done. If he has them posted up, mimeographed, printed in newspapers or published in book form, then the problem becomes indeed a big one, for they can influence many people. And those who produce stereotyped Party writing always seek large audiences. Thus it has become imperative to expose and destroy it.

This speech was delivered by Comrade Mao Tse-tung at a cadres' meeting in Yenan.

Stereotyped Party writing is, moreover, one brand of the "foreign stereotype", which was attacked by Lu Hsun a long time ago.[1] Why then do we call it the Party "eight-legged essay"? Because, besides its foreign flavour, it has some smell of native soil. Perhaps it too can be counted as creative work of a sort! Who says our people have not produced any creative works? Here is one! (*Loud laughter.*)

Stereotyped Party writing has a long history in our Party; particularly during the Agrarian Revolution, it sometimes became quite rampant.

Viewed historically, stereotyped Party writing is a reaction to the May 4th Movement.

During the May 4th Movement, modern-minded people opposed the use of the classical Chinese language and advocated vernacular Chinese, opposed the traditional dogmas and advocated science and democracy, all of which was quite right. The movement then was vigorous and lively, progressive and revolutionary. In those days the ruling classes indoctrinated students with Confucian teachings and compelled the people to venerate all the trappings of Confucianism as religious dogma, and all writers used the classical language. In short, what was written and taught by the ruling classes and their hangers-on was in the nature of stereotyped writing and dogma, both in content and in form. That was the old stereotype and the old dogma. A tremendous achievement of the May 4th Movement was its public exposure of the ugliness of the old stereotype and the old dogma and its call to the people to rise against them. Another great and related achievement was its fight against imperialism, but the struggle against the old stereotype and the old dogma remains one of the great achievements of the May 4th Movement. Later on, however, foreign stereotyped writing and foreign dogma came into being. Running counter to Marxism, certain people in our Party developed the foreign stereotype and dogma into subjectivism, sectarianism and stereotyped Party writing. These are the new stereotype and the new dogma. They have become so deeply ingrained in the minds of many comrades that today we still have a very strenuous job of remoulding to do. Thus we see that the lively, vigorous, progressive and revolutionary movement of the May 4th period which fought the old feudal stereotyped writing and dogma was later turned by some people into its very opposite, giving rise to the new stereotyped writing and dogma. The latter are not lively and vigorous but dead and stiff, not progressive but retrogressive, not revolutionary but obstacles to revolution. That is to say, the foreign stereotyped writing, or stereotyped Party writing, is a reaction to the original nature of the May 4th Movement. The May 4th Movement, however, had its own weaknesses. Many of the leaders lacked the critical spirit of Marxism, and the method they used was generally that of the bourgeoisie, that is, the formalist method. They were quite right in opposing the old stereotype and the old dogma and in advocating science and democracy. But in dealing with current conditions, with history, and with things foreign, they lacked the critical spirit of historical materialism and regarded what was bad as absolutely and wholly bad and what was good as absolutely and wholly good. This formalist approach to problems affected the subsequent course of the movement. In its development, the May 4th Movement divided into two currents. One section inherited its scientific and democratic spirit and transformed it on the basis of Marxism; this is what the Communists and some non-Party Marxists did. Another section took the road of the bourgeoisie; this was the development of formalism towards the Right. But within the Communist Party too the situation was not uniform; there, too, some members deviated and, lacking a firm grasp of Marxism, committed errors of formalism, namely, the errors of subjectivism, sectarianism and stereotyped Party writing. This was the development of formalism towards the "Left". So it can be seen that stereotyped Party writing is no accident, but is, on the one hand, a reaction to the positive elements of the May 4th Movement and, on the other, a legacy, a continuation or development of its negative elements. It is useful for us to understand this point. Just as it was revolutionary and necessary to fight the old stereotyped writing and the old dogmatism during the period of the May 4th Movement, so it is revolutionary and necessary today for us to use Marxism to criticize the new stereotyped writing and the new dogmatism. If there had been no fight against the old stereotype and the old dogmatism during the May 4th period, the minds of the Chinese people would not have been freed from bondage to them, and China would have no hope of freedom and independence. This task was merely begun in the period of the May 4th Movement, and a very great effort — a huge job of work on the road of revolutionary remoulding — is still necessary to enable the whole people to free themselves completely from the domination of the old stereotype and dogmatism. If today we do not oppose the new stereotyped writing and the new dogmatism, the minds of the Chinese people will be fettered by formalism of another kind. If we do not get rid of the poison of stereotyped Party writing and the error of dogmatism found among a section (only a section, of course) of Party comrades, then it will be impossible to arouse a vigorous and lively revolutionary spirit, to eradicate the bad habit of taking a wrong attitude towards Marxism and to disseminate and develop true Marxism;

furthermore, it will be impossible to conduct an energetic struggle against the influence of the old stereotyped writing and dogma among the whole people, and against that of foreign stereotyped writing and dogma among many of the people, and impossible to attain the purpose of demolishing and sweeping away these influences.

Subjectivism, sectarianism and stereotyped Party writing — all three are anti-Marxist and meet the needs not of the proletariat but of the exploiting classes. They are a reflection of petty-bourgeois ideology in our Party. China is a country with a very large petty bourgeoisie and our Party is surrounded by this enormous class; a great number of our Party members come from this class, and when they join the Party they inevitably drag in with them a petty-bourgeois tail, be it long or short. Unless checked and transformed, the fanaticism and one-sidedness of petty-bourgeois revolutionaries can easily engender subjectivism and sectarianism, of which foreign stereotyped writing, or stereotyped Party writing, is one form of expression.

It is not easy to clean out these things and sweep them away. It must be done properly, that is, by taking pains to reason with people. If we reason earnestly and properly, it will be effective. The first thing to do in this reasoning process is to give the patient a good shake-up by shouting at him, "You are ill!" so as to administer a shock and make him break out in a sweat, and then to give him sincere advice on getting treatment.

Let us now analyse stereotyped Party writing and see where its evils lie. Using poison as an antidote to poison, we shall imitate the form of the stereotyped eight-section essay and set forth the following "eight legs", which might be called the eight major indictments.

The first indictment against stereotyped Party writing is that it fills endless pages with empty verbiage. Some of our comrades love to write long articles with no substance, very much like the "foot-bindings of a slattern, long as well as smelly". Why must they write such long and empty articles? There can be only one explanation; they are determined the masses shall not read them. Because the articles are long and empty, the masses shake their heads at the very sight of them. How can they be expected to read them? Such writings are good for nothing except to bluff the naive, among whom they spread bad influences and foster bad habits. On June 22 last year the Soviet Union began waging a gigantic war against aggression, and yet Stalin's speech on July 3 was only the length of an editorial in our *Liberation Daily*. Had any of our gentlemen written that speech, just imagine! It would have run to tens of thousands of words at a minimum. We are in the midst of a war, and we should learn how to write shorter and pithier articles. Although there is as yet no fighting here in Yenan, our troops at the front are daily engaged in battle, and the people in the rear are busy at work. If articles are too long, who will read them? Some comrades at the front, too, like to write long reports. They take pains over writing them and send them here for us to read. But who has the hardihood to read them? If long and empty articles are no good, are short and empty ones any better? They are no good either. We should forbid all empty talk. But the first and foremost task is to throw the long, smelly foot-bindings of the slattern into the dustbin. Some may ask, "Isn't *Capital* very long? What are we to do about that?" The answer is simple, just go on reading it. There is a proverb, "Sing different songs on different mountains"; another runs, "Fit the appetite to the dishes and the dress to the figure". Whatever we do must be done according to actual circumstances, and it is the same with writing articles and making speeches. What we oppose is long-winded and empty stereotyped writing, but we do not mean that everything must necessarily be short in order to be good. True, we need short articles in war time, but above all we need articles that have substance. Articles devoid of substance are the least justifiable and the most objectionable. The same applies to speech-making; we must put an end to all empty, long-winded speeches.

The second indictment against stereotyped Party writing is that it strikes a pose in order to intimidate people. Some stereotyped Party writing is not only long and empty, but also pretentious with the deliberate intention of intimidating people; it carries the worst kind of poison. Writing long-winded and empty articles may be set down to immaturity, but striking a pose to overawe people is not merely immature but downright knavish. Lu Hsun once said in criticism of such people, "Hurling insults and threats is certainly not fighting."[2] What is scientific never fears criticism, for science is truth and fears no refutation. But those who write subjectivist and sectarian articles and speeches in the form of Party stereotypes fear refutation, are very cowardly, and therefore rely on pretentiousness to overawe others, believing that they can thereby silence people and "win the day". Such pretentiousness cannot reflect truth but is an obstacle to truth. Truth does not strike a pose to overawe people but talks and acts honestly and sincerely. Two terms used to appear in the articles and speeches of many comrades, one being "ruthless struggle" and the other "merciless blows". Measures of that kind are entirely necessary against the enemy or against enemy ideology, but to use them against our own comrades is wrong. It often happens that enemies and enemy ideology infiltrate into the Party, as is discussed in Item 4 of the Conclusion of the *History of the Communist Party of the Soviet Union (Bolsheviks), Short Course*. Against these enemies, we must undoubtedly resort to ruthless struggle and merciless blows, because the scoundrels use these very measures against the Party; if we were tolerant of them, we should fall right into their trap. But the same measures should not be used against comrades who occasionally make mistakes; to them we should apply the method of criticism and self-criticism, the method indicated in Item 5 of the Conclusion of the *History of the Communist Party of the Soviet Union (Bolsheviks), Short Course*. The comrades who in the past loudly advocated "ruthless struggle" and "merciless blows" against comrades who occasionally made mistakes did so because, for one thing, they failed to make any analysis of the persons they were dealing with and, for another, they were striking a pose in an effort to intimidate. This method is no good, no matter whom you are dealing with. Against the enemy this tactic of intimidation is utterly useless, and with our own comrades it can only do harm. It is a tactic which the exploiting classes and the *lumpen*-proletariat habitually practise, but for which the proletariat has no use. For the proletariat the sharpest and most effective weapon is a serious and militant scientific attitude. The Communist Party lives by the truth of Marxism-Leninism, by seeking truth from facts, by science, and not by intimidating people. Needless to say, the idea of attaining fame and position for oneself by pretentiousness is even more contemptible. In short, when organizations make decisions and issue instructions and when comrades write articles and make speeches, they must without exception depend on Marxist-Leninist truth and seek to serve

99

a useful purpose. This is the only basis on which victory in the revolution can be achieved; all else is of no avail.

The third indictment against stereotyped Party writing is that it shoots at random, without considering the audience. A few years ago a slogan appeared on the Yenan city wall which read, "Working men and peasants, unite and strive for victory in the War of Resistance Against Japan!" The idea of the slogan was not at all bad, but the character "工" [*kung*, meaning working] in "工人" [*kung jen*, meaning working men], was written as "互", with its perpendicular stroke twisted into a zigzag. How about the character "人" [*jen,* meaning men]? It became "𠆢", with three slanting strokes added to its right leg. The comrade who wrote this was no doubt a disciple of the ancient scholars, but it is rather baffling why he should have written such characters in such a place, on the Yenan city wall, at the time of the War of Resistance. Perhaps he had taken a vow that the common people should not read them; it is difficult to explain otherwise. Communists who really want to do propaganda must consider their audience and bear in mind those who will read their articles and slogans or listen to their speeches and their talk; otherwise they are in effect resolving not to be read or listened to by anyone. Many people often take it for granted that what they write and say can be easily understood by everybody, when it is not so at all. How can people understand them when they write and speak in Party stereotypes? The saying "to play the lute to a cow" implies a gibe at the audience. If we substitute the idea of respect for the audience, the gibe is turned against the player. Why should he strum away without considering his audience? What is worse, he is producing a Party stereotype as raucous as a crow, and yet he insists on cawing at the masses. When shooting an arrow, one must aim at the target; when playing the lute, one must consider the listener; how, then, can one write articles or make speeches without taking the reader or the audience into account? Suppose we want to make friends with a person, whoever he may be, can we become bosom friends if we do not understand each other's hearts, do not know each other's thoughts? It simply will not do for our propaganda workers to rattle on without investigating, studying and analysing their audience.

The fourth indictment against stereotyped Party writing is its drab language that reminds one of a *piehsan*. Like our stereotyped Party writing, the creatures known in Shanghai as "little *piehsan*" are wizened and ugly. If an article or a speech merely rings the changes on a few terms in a classroom tone without a shred of vigour or spirit, is it not rather like a *piehsan*, drab of speech and repulsive in appearance? If someone enters primary school at seven, goes to middle school in his teens, graduates from college in his twenties and never has contact with the masses of the people, he is not to blame if his language is poor and monotonous. But we are revolutionaries working for the masses, and if we do not learn the language of the masses, we cannot work well. At present many of our comrades doing propaganda work make no study of language. Their propaganda is very dull, and few people care to read their articles or listen to their talk. Why do we need to study language and, what is more, spend much effort on it? Because the mastery of language is not easy and requires painstaking effort. First, let us learn language from the masses. The people's vocabulary is rich, vigorous, vivid and expressive of real life. It is because many of us have not mastered language that our articles and speeches contain few vigorous, vivid and effective expressions and resemble not a hale and healthy person, but an emaciated *piehsan,* a mere bag of bones. Secondly, let us absorb what we need from foreign languages. We should not import foreign expressions mechanically or use them indiscriminately, but should absorb what is good and suits our needs. Our current vocabulary has already incorporated many foreign expressions, because the old Chinese vocabulary was inadequate. For instance, today we are holding a meeting of *kanpu* [cadres], and the term *kanpu* is derived from a foreign word. We should continue to absorb many fresh things from abroad, not only progressive ideas but new expressions as well. Thirdly, let us also learn whatever is alive in the classical Chinese language. Since we have not studied classical Chinese hard enough, we have not made full and proper use of much that is still alive in it. Of course, we are resolutely opposed to the use of obsolete expressions or allusions, and that is final; but what is good and still useful should be taken over. Those who are badly infected by stereotyped Party writing do not take pains to study what is useful in the language of the people, in foreign languages, or in classical Chinese, so the masses do not welcome their dry and dull propaganda, and we too have no need for such poor and incompetent propagandists. Who are our propagandists? They include not only teachers, journalists, writers and artists, but all our cadres. Take the military commanders, for instance. Though they make no public statements, they have to talk to the soldiers and have dealings with the people. What is this if not propaganda? Whenever a man speaks to others, he is doing propaganda work. Unless he is dumb, he always has a few words to say. It is therefore imperative that our comrades should all study language.

The fifth indictment against stereotyped Party writing is that it arranges items under a complicated set of headings, as if starting a Chinese pharmacy. Go and take a look at any Chinese pharmacy, and you will see cabinets with numerous drawers, each bearing the name of a drug — toncal, foxglove, rhubarb, saltpetre . . . indeed, everything that should be there. This method has been picked up by our comrades. In their articles and speeches, their books and reports, they use first the big Chinese numerals, second the small Chinese numerals, third the characters for the ten celestial stems, fourth the characters for the twelve earthly branches, and then capital A, B, C, D, then small a, b, c, d, followed by the Arabic numerals, and what not! How fortunate that the ancients and the foreigners created all these symbols for us so that we can start a Chinese pharmacy without the slightest effort. For all its verbiage, an article that bristles with such symbols, that does not pose, analyse or solve problems and that does not take a stand for or against anything is devoid of real content and nothing but a Chinese pharmacy. I am not saying that such symbols as the ten celestial stems, etc., should not be used, but that this kind of approach to problems is wrong. The method borrowed from the Chinese pharmacy, which many of our comrades are very fond of, is really the most crude, infantile and philistine of all. It is a formalist method, classifying things according to their external features instead of their internal relations. If one takes a conglomeration of concepts that are not internally related and arranges them into an article, speech or report simply according to the external features of things, then one is juggling with concepts and may also lead others to indulge in the same sort of game, with the result that they do not use their brains to think over problems and probe into the essence of things, but are satisfied merely to list phenomena in ABCD order. What is a problem? A problem is the contradiction in a thing. Where one has an unresolved contradiction, there one has a problem. Since there is a problem, you have to be for one side and against the other, and you have to pose the problem. To pose the problem, you must first make a preliminary investigation and study of the two basic aspects of the problem or contradiction before you can understand the nature of the contradiction. This is the process of discovering the problem. Preliminary investigation and study can discover the problem, can pose the problem, but cannot as yet solve it. In order to solve the problem it is necessary to make a systematic and thorough investigation and study. This is the process of analysis. In posing the problem too, analysis is needed; otherwise, faced with a chaotic and bewildering mass of phenomena, you will not be able to discern where the problem or contradiction lies. But here, by the process of analysis we mean a process of systematic and thorough analysis. It often happens that although a problem has been posed it cannot be solved because the internal relations of things have not yet been revealed, because this process of systematic and thorough analysis has not yet been carried out; consequently we still cannot see the contours of the problem clearly, cannot make a synthesis and so cannot solve the problem well. If an article or speech is important and meant to give guidance, it ought to pose a particular problem, then analyse it and then make a synthesis pointing to the nature of the problem and providing the method for solving it; in all this, formalist methods are useless. Since infantile, crude, philistine and lazy-minded formalist methods are prevalent in our Party, we must expose them; only thus can everybody learn to use the Marxist method to observe, pose, analyse and solve problems; only thus can we do our work well and only thus can our revolutionary cause triumph.

The sixth indictment against stereotyped Party writing is that it is irresponsible and harms people wherever it appears. All the offences mentioned above are due partly to immaturity and partly to an insufficient sense of responsibility. Let us take washing the face to illustrate the point. We all wash our faces every day, many of us more than once, and inspect ourselves in the mirror afterwards by way of "investigation and study" (*loud laughter*), for fear that something may not be quite right. What a great sense of responsibility! If we wrote articles and made speeches with the same sense of responsibility, we would not be doing badly. Do not present what is not presentable. Always bear in mind that it may influence the thoughts and actions of others. If a man happens not to wash his face for a day or two, that of course is not good, and if after washing he leaves a smudge or two, that too is not so pleasing, but there is no serious danger. It is different with writing articles or making speeches; they are intended solely to influence others. Yet our comrades go about this task casually; this means putting the trivial above the important. Many people write articles and make speeches without prior study or preparation, and after writing an article, they do not bother to go over it several times in the same way as they would examine their faces in the mirror after washing, but instead offhandedly send it to be published. Often the result is "A thousand words from the pen in a stream, but ten thousand *li* away from the theme". Talented though these writers may appear, they actually harm people. This bad habit, this weak sense of responsibility, must be corrected.

The seventh indictment against stereotyped Party writing is that it poisons the whole Party and jeopardizes the revolution. The eighth indictment is that its spread would wreck the country and ruin the people. These two indictments are self-evident and require no elaboration. In other words, if stereotyped Party writing is not transformed but is allowed to develop unchecked, the consequences will be very serious indeed. The poison of subjectivism and sectarianism is hidden in stereotyped Party writing, and if this poison spreads it will endanger both the Party and the country.

The aforesaid eight counts are our call to arms against stereotyped Party writing.

As a form, the Party stereotype is not only unsuitable for expressing the revolutionary spirit but is apt to stifle it. To develop the revolutionary spirit it is necessary to discard stereotyped Party writing and instead to adopt the Marxist-Leninist style of writing, which is vigorous, lively, fresh and forceful. This style of writing has existed for a long time, but is yet to be enriched and spread widely among us. When we have destroyed foreign stereotyped writing and stereotyped Party writing, we can enrich our new style of writing and spread it widely, thereby advancing the Party's revolutionary cause.

The Party stereotype is not only confined to articles and speeches, but is also found in the conduct of meetings. "1. Opening announcement; 2. report; 3. discussion; 4. conclusions; and 5. adjournment." If this rigid procedure is followed at every meeting, large or small, everywhere and every time, is not that another Party stereotype? When "reports" are made at meetings they often go as follows: "1. the international situation; 2. the domestic situation; 3. the Border Region; and 4. our own department"; and the meetings often last from morning till night, with even those having nothing to say taking the floor, as though they would let the others down unless they spoke. In short, there is a disregard for actual conditions and deadly adherence to rigid old forms and habits. Should we not correct all these things too?

Nowadays many people are calling for a transformation to a national, scientific and mass style. That is very good. But "transformation" means thorough change, from top to bottom and inside out. Yet some people who have not made even a slight change are calling for a transformation. I would therefore advise these comrades to begin by making just a little change before they go on to "transform", or else they will remain entangled in dogmatism and stereotyped Party writing. This can be described as having grandiose aims but puny abilities, great ambition but little talent, and it will accomplish nothing. So whoever talks glibly about "transformation to a mass style" while in fact he is stuck fast in his own small circle had better watch out, or some day one of the masses may bump into him along the road and say, "What about all this 'transformation', sir? Can I see a bit of it, please?" and he will be in a fix. If he is not just prating but sincerely wants to transform to a mass style, he must really go among the common people and learn from them, otherwise his "transformation" will remain up in the air. There are some who keep clamouring for transformation to a mass style but cannot speak three sentences in the language of the common people. It shows they are not really determined to learn from the masses. Their minds are still confined to their own small circles.

At this meeting copies of *A Guide to Propaganda,* a pamphlet containing four articles, have been distributed, and I advise our comrades to read and re-read it.

The first piece, composed of excerpts from the *History of the Communist Party of the Soviet Union (Bolsheviks), Short Course,* deals with the way Lenin did propaganda work. It describes, among other things, how Lenin wrote leaflets:

> Under Lenin's guidance, the St. Petersburg League of Struggle for the Emancipation of the Working Class was the first body in Russia that began to *unite Socialism with the working-class movement*. When a strike broke out in some factory, the League of Struggle, which through the members of its circles was kept well posted on the state of affairs in the factories, immediately responded by issuing leaflets and Socialist proclamations. These leaflets exposed the oppression of the workers by the manufacturers, explained how the workers should fight for their interests, and set forth the workers' demands. The leaflets told the plain truth about the ulcers of capitalism, the poverty of the workers, their intolerably hard working day of 12 to 14 hours, and their utter lack of rights. They also put forward appropriate political demands.

Take note, "well posted" and "told the plain truth"! Again:

> With the collaboration of the worker Babushkin, Lenin at the end of 1894 wrote the first agitational leaflet of this kind and an appeal to the workers of the Semyannikov Works in St. Petersburg who were on strike.

To write a leaflet, you must consult with comrades who are well posted on the state of affairs. It was on the basis of such investigation and study that Lenin wrote and worked.

> Every leaflet greatly helped to stiffen the spirit of the workers. They saw that the Socialists were helping and defending them.[3]

Do we agree with Lenin? If we do, we must work in the spirit of Lenin. That is, we must do as Lenin did and not fill endless pages with verbiage, or shoot at random without considering the audience, or become self-opinionated and bombastic.

The second piece is composed of excerpts from Dimitrov's statements at the Seventh World Congress of the Communist International. What did Dimitrov say? He said:

> We must learn to talk to the masses, not in the language of book formulas, but in the language of fighters for the cause of the masses, whose every word, whose every idea reflects the innermost thoughts and sentiments of millions.[4]

And again:

> . . . *the masses cannot assimilate our decisions unless we learn to speak the language which the masses understand.*
>
> We do not always know how to speak simply, concretely, in images which are familiar and intelligible to the masses. We are still unable to refrain from abstract formulas which we have learned by rote. As a matter of fact, if you look through our leaflets, newspapers, resolutions and theses, you will find that they are often written in a language and style so heavy that they are difficult for even our Party functionaries to understand, let alone the rank-and-file workers.[5]

Well? Does not Dimitrov put his finger on our weak spot? Apparently, stereotyped Party writing exists in foreign countries as well as in China, so you can see it is a common disease. (*Laughter.*) In any case, we should cure our own disease quickly in accordance with Comrade Dimitrov's injunction.

Every one of us must make this a law, a Bolshevik law, an elementary rule:

When writing or speaking always have in mind the rank-and-file worker who must understand you, must believe in your appeal and be ready to follow you! You must have in mind those for whom you write, to whom you speak.[6]

This is the prescription made out for us by the Communist International, a prescription that must be followed. Let it be a *law* for us!

The third article, selected from the *Complete Works of Lu Hsun*, is the author's reply to the magazine *The Dipper*,[7] discussing how to write. What did Lu Hsun say? Altogether he set forth eight rules of writing, some of which I shall pick out for comment here.

Rule 1: "Pay close attention to all manner of things; observe more, and if you have observed only a little, then do not write."

What he says is, "pay close attention to all manner of things", not just to one thing or half a thing. He says "observe more", not just take a look or half a look. How about us? Don't we often do exactly the opposite and write after having observed only a little?

Rule 2: "Do not force yourself to write when you have nothing to say."

What about us? Don't we often force ourselves to write a great deal when it is all too clear that there is nothing in our heads? It is sheer irresponsibility to pick up the pen and "force ourselves to write" without investigation or study.

Rule 4: "After writing something, read it over twice at least, and do your utmost to strike out non-essential words, sentences and paragraphs, without the slightest compunction. Rather condense the material for a novel into a sketch, never spin out the material for a sketch into a novel."

Confucius advised, "Think twice",[8] and Han Yu said, "A deed is accomplished through taking thought."[9] That was in ancient times. Today matters have become very complicated, and sometimes it is not even enough to think them over three or four times. Lu Hsun said, "Read it over twice at least." And at most? He did not say, but in my opinion it does no harm to go over an important article more than ten times and to revise it conscientiously before it is published. Articles are the reflection of objective reality, which is intricate and complex and must be studied over and over again before it can be properly reflected; to be slipshod in this respect is to be ignorant of the rudiments of writing.

Rule 6: "Do not coin adjectives or other terms that are intelligible to nobody but yourself."

We have "coined" too many expressions that are "intelligible to nobody". Sometimes a single clause runs to forty or fifty words and is packed with "adjectives or other terms that are intelligible to nobody". Many who never tire of professing to follow Lu Hsun are the very ones who turn their backs on him!

The last piece is taken from the report on how to develop a national style of propaganda, which was adopted at the

Sixth Plenary Session of the Sixth Central Committee of the Communist Party of China. At that session held in 1938, we said that "any talk about Marxism apart from China's specific characteristics is only Marxism in the abstract, Marxism in a vacuum". That is to say, we must oppose all empty talk about Marxism, and Communists living in China must study Marxism by linking it with the realities of the Chinese revolution.

The report said:

Foreign stereotypes must be abolished, there must be less singing of empty, abstract tunes, and dogmatism must be laid to rest; they must be replaced by the fresh, lively Chinese style and spirit which the common people of China love. To separate internationalist content from national form is the practice of those who do not understand the first thing about internationalism. We, on the contrary, must link the two closely. In this matter there are serious errors in our ranks which should be conscientiously overcome.

The abolition of foreign stereotypes was demanded in that report, yet some comrades are still promoting them. Less singing of empty, abstract tunes was demanded, yet some comrades are obstinately singing more. The demand was made that dogmatism be laid to rest, yet some comrades are telling it to get out of bed. In short, many people have let this report which was adopted at the Sixth Plenary Session go in one ear and out of the other, as if wilfully opposed to it.

The Central Committee has now made the decision that we must discard stereotyped Party writing, dogmatism and the like once and for all, and that is why I have come and talked at some length. I hope that comrades will think over and analyse what I have said and that each comrade will also analyse his own particular case. Everyone should carefully examine himself, talk over with his close friends and the comrades around him whatever he has clarified and really get rid of his own defects.

NOTES

[1] Opposition to stereotyped writing, whether old or new, runs all through Lu Hsun's works. The foreign stereotype was developed after the May 4th Movement by some shallow bourgeois and petty-bourgeois intellectuals and, disseminated by them, existed for a long time among revolutionary cultural workers. In a number of essays, Lu Hsun fought against the foreign stereotype as found in their ranks and condemned it in these terms:

A clean sweep should be made of all stereotyped writings, whether old or new. . . . For instance, it is also a kind of stereotype if all one can do is to "hurl insults", "threaten" or even "pass sentence" and merely copy old formulas and apply these indiscriminately to every fact, instead of specifically and concretely using formulas derived from science to interpret the new facts and phenomena which emerge every day. ("A Reply to Chu Hsiu-hsia's Letter", appended to "Giving the Show Away".)

[2] "Hurling Insults and Threats Is Certainly Not Fighting" was the title of an essay written in 1932 and included in the collection *Mixed Dialects* (Lu Hsun, *Complete Works*, Chin. ed., 1957, Vol. V).

[3] See *History of the Communist Party of the Soviet Union (Bolsheviks), Short Course*, Eng. ed., FLPH, Moscow, 1951, pp. 36-37.

[4] Georgi Dimitrov, "Unity of the Working Class Against Fascism", *Selected Articles and Speeches*, Eng. ed., Lawrence & Wishart, London, 1951, pp. 116-17.

[5] *Ibid.*, pp. 132-33.

[6] *Ibid.*, p. 135.

[7] *The Dipper* was a monthly published in 1931 and 1932 by the League of Chinese Left-Wing Writers. "In Reply to the Question Put by *The*

Dipper" is included in the collection *Two Hearts* (Lu Hsun, *Complete Works,* Chin. ed., 1957, Vol. IV).

[8] From *Confucian Analects,* Book V, "Kungyeh Chang".

[9] Han Yu (768-824) was a famous Chinese writer of the Tang Dynasty. In his essay "The Scholar's Apologia" he wrote, "A deed is accomplished through taking thought and fails through lack of thought."

THE UNITED FRONT IN CULTURAL WORK

October 30, 1944

The purpose of all our work is the overthrow of Japanese imperialism. Like Hitler, Japanese imperialism is approaching its doom. But we must continue our efforts, for only so can we achieve its final overthrow. In our work the war comes first, then production, then cultural work. An army without culture is a dull-witted army, and a dull-witted army cannot defeat the enemy.

The culture of the Liberated Areas already has its progressive side, but it still has a backward side. The Liberated Areas already have a new culture, a people's culture, but a good many vestiges of feudalism survive. Among the 1,500,000 people of the Shensi-Kansu-Ningsia Border Region there are more than 1,000,000 illiterates, there are 2,000 practitioners of witchcraft, and the broad masses are still under the influence of superstition. These are enemies inside the minds of the people. It is often more difficult to combat the enemies inside people's minds than to fight Japanese imperialism. We must call on the masses to arise in struggle against their own illiteracy, superstitions and unhygienic

---

This speech was delivered by Comrade Mao Tse-tung at a conference of cultural and educational workers of the Shensi-Kansu-Ningsia Border Region.

habits. For this struggle a broad united front is indispensable. And this united front has to be particularly broad in a place like the Shensi-Kansu-Ningsia Border Region, which has a sparse population, poor communications and a low cultural base to start from and in addition is fighting a war. Hence, in our education we must have not only regular primary and secondary schools but also scattered, irregular village schools, newspaper-reading groups and literacy classes. Not only must we have schools of the modern type but we must also utilize and transform the old-style village schools. In the arts, we must have not only modern drama but also the Shensi opera and the *yangko* dance.[1] Not only must we have new Shensi operas and new *yangko* dances, but we must also utilize and gradually transform the old opera companies and the old *yangko* troupes, which comprise 90 per cent of all *yangko* troupes. This approach is even more necessary in the field of medicine. In the Shensi-Kansu-Ningsia Border Region the human and animal mortality rates are both very high, and at the same time many people still believe in witchcraft. In such circumstances, to rely solely on modern doctors is no solution. Of course, modern doctors have advantages over doctors of the old type, but if they do not concern themselves with the sufferings of the people, do not train doctors for the people, do not unite with the thousand and more doctors and veterinarians of the old type in the Border Region and do not help them to make progress, then they will actually be helping the witch doctors and showing indifference to the high human and animal mortality rates. There are two principles for the united front: the first is to unite, and the second is to criticize, educate and transform. In the united front, capitalizationism is wrong, and so is sectarianism with its exclusiveness and contempt for others. Our task is to unite with all intellectuals, artists and doctors of the old type who can be useful, to help them, convert them and transform them. In order to transform them, we must first unite with them. If we do it properly, they will welcome our help.

Our culture is a people's culture; our cultural workers must serve the people with great enthusiasm and devotion, and they must link themselves with the masses, not divorce themselves from the masses. In order to do so, they must act in accordance with the needs and wishes of the masses. All work done for the masses must start from their needs and not from the desire of any individual, however well-intentioned. It often happens that objectively the masses need a certain change, but subjectively they are not yet conscious of the need, not yet willing or determined to make the change. In such cases, we should wait patiently. We should not make the change until, through our work, most of the masses have become conscious of the need and are willing and determined to carry it out. Otherwise we shall isolate ourselves from the masses. Unless they are conscious and willing, any kind of work that requires their participation will turn out to be a mere formality and will fail. The saying "Haste does not bring success" does not mean that we should not make haste, but that we should not be impetuous; impetuosity leads only to failure. This is true in any kind of work, and particularly in the cultural and educational work the aim of which is to transform the thinking of the masses. There are two principles here: one is the actual needs of the masses rather than what we fancy they need, and the other is the wishes of the masses, who must make up their own minds instead of our making up their minds for them.

NOTES

[1] The *yangko* is a folk dance popular in northern China.

THE CHIEF CONCERN OF CHINA'S CULTURAL MOVEMENT

April 24, 1945

It is the peasants who are the chief concern of China's cultural movement at the present stage. If the 360 million peasants are left out, do not the "elimination of illiteracy", "popularization of education", "literature and art for the masses" and "public health" become largely empty talk?

In saying this, I am of course not ignoring the political, economic and cultural importance of the rest of the people numbering about 90 million, and in particular am not ignoring the working class, which is politically the most conscious and therefore qualified to lead the whole revolutionary movement. Let there be no misunderstanding.

From *On Coalition Government*

THE PROBLEM OF CULTURE, EDUCATION AND THE INTELLECTUALS

April 24, 1945

The calamities brought upon the Chinese people by foreign and feudal oppression also affect our national culture. The progressive cultural and educational institutions and progressive cultural workers and educators have particularly suffered. To sweep away foreign and feudal oppression and build a new-democratic China, we need large numbers of educators and teachers for the people, and also people's scientists, engineers, technicians, doctors, journalists, writers, men of letters, artists and rank-and-file cultural workers. They must be imbued with the spirit of serving the people and must work hard. Provided they serve the people creditably, all intellectuals should be esteemed and regarded as valuable national and social assets. The problem of the intellectuals becomes particularly important in China because the country is culturally backward as a result of foreign and feudal oppression and because intellectuals are urgently needed in the people's struggle for liberation. The numerous revolutionary intellectuals have played a very great role in the people's struggle for liberation in the past half-century, and especially since the May 4th Movement of 1919 and in the eight years of the anti-Japanese war. They will play an even greater role in the struggles to come. Therefore, the task of a people's government is systematically to develop all kinds of intellectually equipped cadres from among the ranks of the people and at the same time take care to unite with and re-educate all the useful intellectuals already available.

The elimination of illiteracy among 80 per cent of the population is a vital task for the new China.

Proper and firm steps should be taken to eliminate all enslaving feudal and fascist culture and education.

Vigorous action should be taken to prevent and cure endemic and other diseases among the people and to expand the people's medical and health services.

The old type of cultural and educational workers and doctors should be given suitable re-education so that they can acquire a new outlook and new methods to serve the people.

The Chinese people's culture and education should be new-democratic, that is to say, China should establish her own new national, scientific and mass culture and education.

As for foreign culture, it would be a wrong policy to shut it out, rather we should as far as possible draw on what is progressive in it for use in the development of China's new culture; it would also be wrong to copy it blindly, rather we should draw on it critically to meet the actual needs of the Chinese people. The new culture created in the Soviet Union should be a model for us in building our people's culture. Similarly, ancient Chinese culture should neither be totally rejected nor blindly copied, but should be accepted discriminatingly so as to help the progress of China's new culture.

From *On Coalition Government*

A TALK TO THE EDITORIAL STAFF OF THE *SHANSI-SUIYUAN DAILY*

April 2, 1948

Our policy must be made known not only to the leaders and to the cadres but also to the broad masses. Questions concerning policy should as a rule be given publicity in the Party papers or periodicals. We are now carrying out the reform of the land system. The policies on land reform should be published in the papers and broadcast on the radio so that the broad masses all know them. Once the masses know the truth and have a common aim, they will work together with one heart. This is like fighting a battle; to win a battle the fighters as well as the officers must be of one heart. After the troops in northern Shensi went through training and consolidation and poured out their grievances against the old social order, the fighters heightened their political consciousness and became clear on why they were fighting and how they should fight; every one of them rolled up his sleeves for battle, their morale was very high and as soon as they went into action they won a victory. When the masses are of one heart, everything becomes easy. A basic principle of Marxism-Leninism is to enable the masses to know their own interests and unite to fight for their own interests. The role and power of the newspapers consists in their ability to bring the Party programme, the Party line, the Party's general and specific policies, its tasks and methods of work before the masses in the quickest and most extensive way.

There are people in our leading organs in some places who think that it is enough for the leaders alone to know the Party's policies and that there is no need to let the masses know them. This is one of the basic reasons why some of our work cannot be done well. For over twenty years our Party has carried on mass work every day, and for the past dozen years it has talked about the mass line every day. We have always maintained that the revolution must rely on the masses of the people, on everybody's taking a hand, and have opposed relying merely on a few persons issuing orders. The mass line, however, is still not being thoroughly carried out in the work of some comrades; they still rely solely on a handful of people working coolly and quietly by themselves. One reason is that, whatever they do, they are always reluctant to explain it to the people they lead and that they do not understand why or how to give play to the initiative and creative energy of those they lead. Subjectively, they too want everyone to take a hand in the work, but they do not let other people know what is to be done or how to do it. That being the case, how can everyone be expected to get moving and how can anything be done well? To solve this problem the basic thing is, of course, to carry out ideological education on the mass line, but at the same time we must teach these comrades many concrete methods of work. One such method is to make full use of the newspapers. To run a newspaper well, to make it interesting and absorbing, to give correct publicity in the newspapers to the Party's general and specific policies and to strengthen the Party's ties with the masses through the newspapers — this is an important question of principle in our Party's work which is not to be taken lightly.

You comrades are newspapermen. Your job is to educate the masses, to enable the masses to know their own interests, their own tasks and the Party's general and specific policies. Running a newspaper is like all other work, it must be done conscientiously if it is to be done well, if it is to be lively. With our newspapers, too, we must rely on everybody, on the masses of the people, on the whole Party to run them, not merely on a few persons working behind closed doors. Our papers talk about the mass line every day, yet frequently the mass line is not carried out in the work of the newspaper office itself. For instance, misprints often crop up in the papers simply because their elimination has not been tackled as a serious job. If we apply the method of the mass line, then when misprints appear, we should assemble the entire staff of the paper to discuss nothing but this matter, tell them clearly what the mistakes are, explain why they occur and how they can be got rid of and ask everyone to give the matter serious attention. After this has been done three times, or five times, such mistakes can certainly be overcome. This is true of small matters, and of big matters, too.

To be good at translating the Party's policy into action of the masses, to be good at getting not only the leading cadres but also the broad masses to understand and master every movement and every struggle we launch — this is an art of Marxist-Leninist leadership. It is also the dividing line that determines whether or not we make mistakes in our work. If we tried to go on the offensive when the masses are not yet awakened, that would be adventurism. If we insisted on leading the masses to do anything against their will, we would certainly fail. If we did not advance when the masses demand advance, that would be Right opportunism. Chen Tu-hsiu's opportunist error[1] consisted precisely in lagging behind the awakening of the masses, being unable to lead the masses forward and even opposing their forward march. There are many comrades who still don't understand these questions. Our papers should propagate these ideas well so that everyone can understand them.

To teach the masses, newspaper workers should first of all learn from the masses. You comrades are all intellectuals. Intellectuals are often ignorant and often have little or no experience in practical matters. You can't quite understand the pamphlet *How to Differentiate the Classes in the Rural Areas*[2] issued in 1933; on this point, the peasants are more than a match for you, for they understand it fully as soon as they are told about it. Over 180 peasants in two districts of Kuohsien County met for five days and settled many problems concerning the distribution of land. If your editorial department were to discuss those problems, I am afraid you would discuss them for two weeks without settling them. The reason is quite simple; you do not understand those problems. To change from lack of understanding to understanding, one must do things and see things; that is learning. Comrades working on the newspapers should go out by turns to take part in mass work, in land reform work for a time; that is very necessary. When not going out to participate in mass work, you should hear a great deal and read a great deal about the mass movements and devote time and effort to the study of such material. Our slogan in training troops is, "Officers teach soldiers, soldiers teach officers and soldiers teach each other". The fighters have a lot of practical combat experience. The officers should learn from the fighters, and when they have made other people's experience their own, they will become more capable. Comrades working on the newspapers, too, should constantly study the material coming from below, gradually enrich their practical knowledge and become experienced. Only thus will you be able to do your work well, will you be able to shoulder your task of educating the masses.

The *Shansi-Suiyuan Daily* made very great progress following the conference of secretaries of prefectural Party committees last June. Then the paper was rich in content, sharp, pungent and vigorous; it reflected the great mass struggles, it spoke for the masses. I liked reading it very much. But since January this year, when we began to correct "Left" deviations, your paper seems to have lost some of its spirit; it is not clear-cut enough, not pungent enough, has become less informative and does not have much appeal for the reader. Now you are examining your work and summing up your experience; this is very good. When you have summed up your experience in combating Right and "Left" deviations and become more clear-headed, your work will improve.

The struggle against Right deviations waged by the *Shansi-Suiyuan Daily* from last June on was completely correct. In that struggle you did a very conscientious job and fully reflected the actual situation in the mass movement. You made comments, in the form of editorial notes, on the viewpoints and materials which you regarded as wrong. There were shortcomings too in some of your later comments, but the conscientious spirit was good. Your shortcomings lay chiefly in drawing the bow-string much too tight. If a bow-string is too taut, it will snap. The ancients said, "The principle of Kings Wen and Wu was to alternate tension with relaxation."[3] Now "relax" a bit and the comrades will become more clear-headed. You achieved successes in your work, but there were also shortcomings, mainly "Left" deviations. Now you are making an over-all summing-up and, after correcting the "Left" deviations, you will achieve greater successes.

When we are correcting deviations, some people look on the work of the past as utterly fruitless and all wrong. That is not right. These people fail to see that the Party has led a huge number of peasants to obtain land, overthrown feudalism, consolidated the Party organizations and improved the cadres' style of work, and that now it has also corrected the "Left" deviations and educated the cadres and masses. Are all these not great achievements? We should be analytical with regard to our work and the undertakings of the masses, and should not negate everything. In the past "Left" deviations arose because people had no experience. Without experience it is hard to avoid mistakes. From inexperience to experience, one must go through a process. Through the struggles against the Right and "Left" deviations in the short period since June last year, people have come to understand what struggle against Right deviations means and what struggle against "Left" deviations means. Without this process, people would not understand.

After you have examined your work and summed up your experience, I am sure that your paper will be run even better. You must retain the former merits of your paper — it should be sharp, pungent and clear-cut, and it should be run conscientiously. We must firmly uphold the truth, and truth requires a clear-cut stand. We Communists have always disdained to conceal our views. Newspapers run by our Party and all the propaganda work of our Party should be vivid, clear-cut and sharp and should never mutter and mumble.   That is the militant style proper to us, the revolutionary proletariat.   Since we want to teach the people to know the truth and arouse them to fight for their own emancipation, we need this militant style.   A blunt knife draws no blood.

NOTES

[1] Chen Tu-hsiu was a radical democrat around the time of the May 4th Movement. Later, under the influence of the October Socialist Revolution he became one of the founders of the Chinese Communist Party. For six years after the founding of the Party he held the leading position in the Central Committee. His thinking had long been strongly Rightist. In the latter part of the 1924-27 revolution, it developed into a line of capitulationism. The capitulationists represented by Chen Tu-hsiu "voluntarily gave up the Party's leadership of the peasant masses, urban petty bourgeoisie and middle bourgeoisie, and in particular gave up the Party's leadership of the armed forces, thus causing the defeat of the revolution". ("The Present Situation and Our Tasks", *Selected Works of Mao Tse-tung*, Eng. ed., Foreign Languages Press, Peking, 1961, Vol. IV, p. 171.) After the defeat of 1927 Chen Tu-hsiu and a handful of other capitulationists lost faith in the future of the revolution and became liquidationists. They took a reactionary Trotskyite stand and formed a small anti-Party group together with the Trotskyites. Consequently Chen Tu-hsiu was expelled from the Party in November 1929. He died in 1942.

[2] See "How to Differentiate the Classes in the Rural Areas", *Selected Works of Mao Tse-tung*, Eng. ed., FLP, Peking, 1965, Vol. I, pp. 137-39.

[3] From the *Book of Rites*, "Miscellaneous Records", Part II. "Kings Wen and Wu could not keep a bow in permanent tension without relaxation. Nor would they leave it in a permanent state of relaxation without tension. The principle of Kings Wen and Wu was to alternate tension with relaxation." Wen and Wu were the first two kings of the Chou Dynasty (12th-3rd century B.C.).

WHAT TO PRAISE AND WHAT TO CONDEMN

1951

In the view of many writers history develops not by the replacement of the old by the new, but by the exertion of every effort to preserve the old from extinction, not by class struggle to overthrow the reactionary feudal rulers who had to be overthrown, but by the negation of the class struggle of the oppressed and their submission to these rulers, in the manner of Wu Hsun.[1] Our writers have not studied history to ascertain who were the enemies oppressing the Chinese people, and whether there is anything praiseworthy in those who submitted to these enemies and served them. Moreover, they have not tried to find out what new forms of social economy, new class forces, new personalities and ideas have appeared in China and struggled against the old forms of social economy and their superstructure (politics, culture, etc.) in the century and more since the Opium War of 1840, and they have accordingly failed to determine what is to be commended and praised, what is not to be commended and praised, and what is to be condemned.

This passage from the *Renmin Ribao* (*People's Daily*) editorial of May 20, 1951, "Give Serious Attention to the Discussion of the Film, *Life of Wu Hsun*", was added by Comrade Mao Tse-tung when going over the draft editorial.

NOTES

[1] Wu Hsun (1838-95) who started as a beggar, became a rich money-lender and landlord by fawning on the feudal ruling class and fleecing the working people. At a time when the class struggle was sharp and the peasant revolution was surging forward, he went round "begging for funds to establish schools". With the approval and support of the landlord class and the officials, he set up "free schools" to serve the feudal rule. Dressed as a beggar and under the pretext of establishing these schools, in fact he spread the reactionary, decadent feudal culture and morality to prevent the people from in any way touching the feudal economic base and its superstructure.

ON LITERARY STYLE

1955

We wish to thank the anonymous author of this article. Brimming over with enthusiasm and writing in a lively style, he gives a detailed description of the process of building co-operatives in one district. This is no small contribution to the cause of agricultural co-operation throughout the country. We hope every province, prefecture and county will provide one or more articles like this.

> Introductory note to "The Party Secretary Takes the Lead and All the Party Members Help Run the Co-operatives", *The Socialist Upsurge in China's Countryside*

The method described in this article, "make four comparisons and five calculations", is a fine one for showing the peasants which system is good and which is bad and enabling people to understand at once. It is most convincing. It is quite unlike the method of those comrades who are incompetent propagandists and merely say, "Either you follow the road of the Communist Party, or you follow the road of Chiang Kai-shek", trying to put pressure on the audience by name-calling without producing anything substantial. This method takes the local peasants' own experience and provides them with a detailed analysis. Hence its great power to convince.

Introductory note to "Strengthening the Co-operative — a Good Example", *The Socialist Upsurge in China's Countryside*

This article is very well done and deserves to be recommended to all Party and Youth League committees at the county and district levels and to all township branches; all our co-operatives should follow the example it sets. The writer understands the Party's line and speaks straight to the point. Also his style is good; it is readily intelligible and does not smack of stereotyped Party writing. Here, we should like to point out to the reader how fond of Party stereotypes in writing many comrades are, with the result that their articles are lifeless and dull and give the reader a headache. Caring little for grammar or rhetoric, they relish a style which is a cross between the literary and the colloquial, verbose and rambling in one place and as elliptical and archaic as possible in another, as though they were deliberately trying to make the reader suffer. Originally, a good many of the more than 170 articles in this book were badly tainted with stereotyped Party writing. Only after several editings have they become fairly readable. Even so, a few are still obscure and difficult to understand. They have been included because of the importance of their content. How many years will it be before we see fewer of these headachy Party stereotypes! Comrades who edit our newspapers and periodicals should pay attention to this question, demand from the writers articles that are vivid and readable, and personally help them to improve their writings.

Introductory note to "Political Work in the Co-operatives", *The Socialist Upsurge in China's Countryside*

ON "LET A HUNDRED FLOWERS BLOSSOM, LET A HUNDRED SCHOOLS OF THOUGHT CONTEND"

February 27, 1957

"Let a hundred flowers blossom, let a hundred schools of thought contend" and "long-term coexistence and mutual supervision" — how did these slogans come to be put forward? They were put forward in the light of China's specific conditions, on the basis of the recognition that various kinds of contradictions still exist in socialist society, and in response to the country's urgent need to speed up its economic and cultural development. Letting a hundred flowers blossom and a hundred schools of thought contend is the policy for promoting the progress of the arts and the sciences and a flourishing socialist culture in our land. Different forms and styles in art should develop freely and different schools in science should contend freely. We think that it is harmful to the growth of art and science if administrative measures are used to impose one particular style of art or school of thought and to ban another. Questions of right and wrong in the arts and sciences should be settled through free discussion in artistic and scientific circles and through practical work in these fields. They should not be settled in summary fashion. A period of trial is often needed to determine whether something is right or wrong. Throughout history, new and correct things have often failed at the outset to win recognition from the majority of people and have had to develop by twists and turns in struggle. Often correct and good things have first been regarded not as fragrant flowers but as poisonous weeds. Copernicus' theory of the solar system and Darwin's theory of evolution were once dismissed as erroneous and had to win through over bitter opposition. Chinese history offers many similar examples. In a socialist society, conditions for the growth of the new are radically different from and far superior to those in the old society. Nevertheless, it still often happens that new, rising forces are held back and rational proposals constricted. Moreover, the growth of new things may be hindered in the absence of deliberate suppression simply through lack of discernment. It is therefore necessary to be careful about questions of right and wrong in the arts and sciences, to encourage free discussion and avoid hasty conclusions. We believe that such an attitude can help to ensure a relatively smooth development of the arts and sciences.

Marxism, too, has developed through struggle. At the beginning, Marxism was subjected to all kinds of attack and regarded as a poisonous weed. It is still being attacked and is still regarded as a poisonous weed in many parts of the world. In the socialist countries, it enjoys a different position. But non-Marxist and, moreover, anti-Marxist ideologies exist even in these countries. In China, although in the main socialist transformation has been completed with respect to the system of ownership, and although the large-scale and turbulent class struggles of the masses characteristic of the previous revolutionary periods have in the main come to an end, there are still remnants of the overthrown landlord and comprador classes, there is still a bourgeoisie, and the remoulding of the petty bourgeoisie has only just started. The class struggle is by no means over. The class struggle between the proletariat and the bourgeoisie, the class struggle between the different political forces, and the class struggle in the ideological field between the proletariat and the bourgeoisie will continue to be long and tortuous and at times will even become very acute. The proletariat seeks to transform the world according to its own world outlook, and so does the bourgeoisie. In this respect, the question of which will win out, socialism or capitalism, is still not really settled. Marxists are still a minority among the entire population as well as among the intellectuals. Therefore, Marxism must still develop through struggle. Marxism can develop only through struggle, and not only is this true of the past and the present, it is necessarily true of the future as well. What is correct invariably develops in the course of struggle with what is wrong. The true, the good and the beautiful always exist by contrast with the false, the evil and the ugly, and grow in struggle with the latter. As soon as a wrong thing is rejected and a particular truth accepted by mankind, new truths begin their struggle with new errors. Such struggles will never end. This is the law of development of truth and, naturally, of Marxism as well.

It will take a fairly long period of time to decide the issue in the ideological struggle between socialism and capitalism in our country. The reason is that the influence of the bourgeoisie and of the intellectuals who come from the old society will remain in our country for a long time to come, and so will their class ideology. If this is not sufficiently understood, or is not understood at all, the gravest mistakes will be made and the necessity of waging the struggle in the ideological field will be ignored. Ideological struggle is not like other forms of struggle. The only method to be used in this struggle is that of painstaking reasoning and not crude coercion. Today, socialism is in an advantageous position in the ideological struggle. The main power of the state is in the hands of the working people led by the proletariat. The Communist Party is strong and its prestige stands high. Although there are defects and mistakes in our work, every fair-minded person can see that we are loyal to the people, that we are both determined and able to build up our motherland together with them, and that we have already achieved great successes and will achieve still greater ones. The vast majority of the bourgeoisie and intellectuals who come from the old society are patriotic and are willing to serve their flourishing socialist motherland; they know they will be helpless and have no bright future to look forward to if they turn away from the socialist cause and from the working people led by the Communist Party.

People may ask, since Marxism is accepted as the guiding ideology by the majority of the people in our country, can it be criticized? Certainly it can. Marxism is scientific truth and fears no criticism. If it did, and if it could be overthrown by criticism, it would be worthless. In fact, aren't the idealists criticizing Marxism every day and in every way? Aren't those who harbour bourgeois and petty-bourgeois ideas and do not wish to change — aren't they also criticizing Marxism in every way? Marxists should not be afraid of criticism from any quarter. Quite the contrary, they need to temper and develop themselves and win new positions in the teeth of criticism and in the storm and stress of struggle. Fighting against wrong ideas is like being vaccinated — a man develops greater immunity from disease as a result of vaccination. Plants raised in hot-houses are un-likely to be sturdy. Carrying out the policy of letting a hundred flowers blossom and a hundred schools of thought contend will not weaken but strengthen the leading position of Marxism in the ideological field.

What should our policy be towards non-Marxist ideas? As far as unmistakable counter-revolutionaries and saboteurs of the socialist cause are concerned, the matter is easy: we simply deprive them of their freedom of speech. But in-correct ideas among the people are quite a different matter. Will it do to ban such ideas and deny them any opportunity for expression? Certainly not. It is not only futile but very harmful to use summary methods in dealing with ideo-logical questions among the people, with questions concerned with man's mental world. You may ban the expression of wrong ideas, but the ideas will still be there. On the other hand, if correct ideas are pampered in hot-houses without being exposed to the elements or immunized from disease, they will not win out against erroneous ones. Therefore, it is only by employing the method of discussion, criticism and reasoning that we can really foster correct ideas and over-come wrong ones, and that we can really settle issues.

Inevitably, the bourgeoisie and petty bourgeoisie will give expression to their own ideologies. Inevitably, they will stubbornly express themselves on political and ideological questions by every possible means. You cannot expect them to do otherwise. We should not use the method of sup-pression and prevent them from expressing themselves, but should allow them to do so and at the same time argue with them and direct appropriate criticism at them. We must undoubtedly criticize wrong ideas of every description. It certainly would not be right to refrain from criticism, look on while wrong ideas spread unchecked and allow them to monopolize the field. Mistakes must be criticized and poisonous weeds fought wherever they crop up. However, such criticism should not be dogmatic, and the metaphysical method should not be used, but efforts should be made to apply the dialectical method. What is needed is scientific analysis and convincing argument. Dogmatic criticism settles nothing. We are against poisonous weeds of any kind, but we must carefully distinguish between what is really a poisonous weed and what is really a fragrant flower. Together with the masses of the people, we must learn to differentiate carefully between the two and to use correct methods to fight the poisonous weeds.

At the same time as we criticize dogmatism, we must direct our attention to criticizing revisionism. Revisionism, or Right opportunism, is a bourgeois trend of thought that is even more dangerous than dogmatism. The revisionists, the Right opportunists, pay lip-service to Marxism; they too attack "dogmatism". But what they are really attacking is the quintessence of Marxism. They oppose or distort materialism and dialectics, oppose or try to weaken the people's democratic dictatorship and the leading role of the Communist Party, and oppose or try to weaken socialist transformation and socialist construction. After the basic victory of the socialist revolution in our country, there are still a number of people who vainly hope to restore the capitalist system and fight the working class on every front, including the ideological one. And their right-hand men in this struggle are the revisionists.

At first glance, the two slogans — let a hundred flowers blossom and let a hundred schools of thought contend — have no class character; the proletariat can turn them to account, and so can the bourgeoisie or other people. But different classes, strata and social groups each have their own views on what are fragrant flowers and what are poisonous weeds. What then, from the point of view of the broad masses of the people, should be the criteria today for distinguishing fragrant flowers from poisonous weeds? In the political life of our people, how should right be distinguished from wrong in one's words and actions? On the basis of the principles of our Constitution, the will of the overwhelming majority of our people and the common political positions which have been proclaimed on various occasions by our political parties and groups, we consider that, broadly speaking, the criteria should be as follows:

(1) Words and actions should help to unite, and not divide, the people of our various nationalities.

(2) They should be beneficial, and not harmful, to socialist transformation and socialist construction.

(3) They should help to consolidate, and not undermine or weaken, the people's democratic dictatorship.

(4) They should help to consolidate, and not undermine or weaken, democratic centralism.

(5) They should help to strengthen, and not discard or weaken, the leadership of the Communist Party.

(6) They should be beneficial, and not harmful, to international socialist unity and the unity of the peace-loving people of the world.

Of these six criteria, the most important are the socialist path and the leadership of the Party. These criteria are put forward not to hinder but to foster the free discussion of questions among the people. Those who disapprove of these criteria can still put forward their own views and argue their case. However, since the majority of the people have clear-cut criteria to go by, criticism and self-criticism can be conducted along proper lines, and the criteria can be applied to people's words and actions to determine whether they are right or wrong, whether they are fragrant flowers or poisonous weeds. These are political criteria. Naturally, in judging the validity of scientific theories or assessing the aesthetic value of works of art, additional pertinent criteria are needed. But these six political criteria are applicable to all activities in the arts and the sciences. In a socialist country like ours, can there possibly be any useful scientific or artistic activity which runs counter to these political criteria?

The views set out above are based on China's specific historical conditions. Conditions vary in different socialist countries and with different Communist Parties. Therefore, we do not maintain that other countries and Parties should or must follow the Chinese way.

From *On the Correct Handling of Contradictions Among the People*

SPEECH AT THE CHINESE COMMUNIST PARTY'S NATIONAL CONFERENCE ON PROPAGANDA WORK

March 12, 1957

Comrades! Our conference[1] has gone very well. Many questions have been raised during the conference and we have learned about many things. I shall now make a few remarks on questions the comrades have been discussing.

We are living in a period of great social change. Chinese society has been going through great changes for a long time. The War of Resistance Against Japan was one period of great change and the War of Liberation another. But the present change is much more profound in character than the earlier ones. We are now building socialism. Hundreds of millions of people are taking part in the movement for socialist transformation. Class relations are changing throughout the country. The petty bourgeoisie in agriculture and handicrafts and the bourgeoisie in industry and commerce have both undergone a change. The social and economic system has been changed; individual economy has been transformed into collective economy, and capitalist private ownership is being transformed into socialist public ownership. Changes of such magnitude are of course reflected in people's minds. Man's social being determines his consciousness. People of different classes, strata and social groups react differently to the great changes in our social system. The masses eagerly support them, for life itself has confirmed that socialism is the only way out for China. Overthrowing the old social system and establishing a new one, the system of socialism, is a great struggle, a great change in the social system and in men's relations with each other. It should be said that the situation is basically sound. But the new social system has only just been established and requires time for its consolidation. It must not be assumed that the new system can be completely consolidated the moment it is established, for that is impossible. It has to be consolidated step by step. To achieve its ultimate consolidation, it is necessary not only to bring about the socialist industrialization of the country and persevere in the socialist revolution on the economic front, but to carry on constant and arduous socialist revolutionary struggles and socialist education on the political and ideological fronts. Moreover, various contributory international factors are required. In China the struggle to consolidate the socialist system, the struggle to decide whether socialism or capitalism will prevail, will still take a long historical period. But we should all realize that the new system of socialism will unquestionably be consolidated. We can assuredly build a socialist state with modern industry, modern agriculture, and modern science and culture. This is the first point I want to make.

Secondly, let us consider the situation regarding the intellectuals in our country. No accurate statistics are available on the number of intellectuals in China. It is estimated that there are about five million of all kinds, including both higher and ordinary intellectuals. Of these five million the overwhelming majority are patriotic, love our People's Republic, and are willing to serve the people and the socialist state. A small number do not quite like socialism and are not very happy. They are still sceptical about socialism, but they are patriotic when it comes to facing imperialism. The number of intellectuals who are hostile to our state is very small. They do not like our state, *i.e.*, the dictatorship of the proletariat, and yearn for the old society. Whenever there is an opportunity, they will stir up trouble and attempt to overthrow the Communist Party and restore the old China. As between the proletarian and the bourgeois roads, as between the socialist and the capitalist roads, these people stubbornly choose to follow the latter. In fact this road is impossible, and in fact, therefore, they are ready to capitulate to imperialism, feudalism and bureaucrat-capitalism. Such people are to be found in political circles and in industrial and commercial, cultural and educational, scientific and technological and religious circles, and they are extremely reactionary. They account for only 1 or 2 or 3 per cent of the five million intellectuals. The overwhelming majority, or well over 90 per cent, of the total of five million, support the socialist system in varying degrees. Many of them are not yet quite clear on how to work under socialism and on how to understand, handle and solve many new problems.

As far as the attitude of the five million intellectuals towards Marxism is concerned, one may say that over 10 per cent, comprising the Communists and sympathizers, are relatively familiar with Marxism and take a firm stand — the stand of the proletariat. Among the total of five million, they are a minority, but they are the nucleus and a powerful force. The majority have the desire to study Marxism and have already learned a little, but they are not yet familiar with it. Some of them still have doubts, their stand is not yet firm and they vacillate in moments of stress. This sec-

144

tion of intellectuals, constituting the majority of the five million, is still in an intermediate state. The number who strongly oppose Marxism, or are hostile to it, is very small. Some people actually disagree with Marxism, although they do not openly say so. There will be people of this sort for a long time to come, and we should allow them to disagree. Take some of the idealists for example. They may support the political and economic system of socialism but disagree with the Marxist world outlook. The same holds true for the patriotic people in religious circles. They are theists and we are atheists. We cannot force them to accept the Marxist world outlook. In short, the attitude of the five million intellectuals towards Marxism may be summed up as follows: Those who support Marxism and are relatively familiar with it are a minority, those who oppose it are also a minority, and the majority support Marxism but are not familiar with it, and support it in varying degrees. Here the stands taken are of three different kinds — resolute, wavering and antagonistic. And this situation will admittedly continue for a long time to come. If we fail to recognize this fact, we shall make too great a demand on others and at the same time set ourselves too small a task. Our comrades in propaganda work have the task of disseminating Marxism. This has to be done gradually and done well, so that people willingly accept it. We cannot force people to accept Marxism, we can only persuade them. If over a period of several five-year plans a fairly large number of our intellectuals accept Marxism and acquire a fairly good grasp of it through their actual work and life, through the practice of class struggle, production and scientific activity, that will be fine. And that is what we hope will happen.

Thirdly, there is the question of the remoulding of the intellectuals. Ours is a culturally undeveloped country. For a vast country like ours, five million intellectuals are too few. Without intellectuals our work cannot be done well, and we should therefore do a good job of uniting with them. Socialist society mainly comprises three sections of people, the workers, the peasants and the intellectuals. Intellectuals are mental workers. Their work is in the service of the people, that is, in the service of the workers and the peasants. As far as the majority of intellectuals are concerned, they can serve the new China as they did the old, and serve the proletariat as they did the bourgeoisie. When the intellectuals served the old China, the left wing resisted, the intermediate section wavered, and only the right wing was resolute. Now, when it comes to serving the new society, the situation is reversed. The left wing is resolute, the intermediate section wavers (this wavering in the new society is different from that in the old society), and the right wing resists. Moreover, intellectuals are educators. Our newspapers are educating the people every day. Our writers and artists, scientists and technicians, professors and teachers are all educating students, educating the people. Being educators and teachers, they themselves must first be educated. And all the more so in the present period of great change in the social system. They have had some Marxist education in the last few years, and some have studied very hard and made great progress. But the majority still have a long way to go before they can completely replace the bourgeois world outlook with the proletarian world outlook. Some people have read a few Marxist books and think themselves quite learned, but what they have read has not penetrated, has not struck root in their minds, so that they do not know how to use it and their class feelings remain as of old. Others are very conceited and having learned some book-phrases, think themselves terrific and are very cocky; but whenever a storm blows up, they take a stand very different from that of the workers and the majority of the peasants. They waver while the latter stand firm, they equivocate while the latter are forthright. Hence it is wrong to assume that people who educate others no longer need to be educated and no longer need to study, or that socialist remoulding means remoulding others — the landlords, the capitalists and the individual producers — but not the intellectuals. The intellectuals, too, need remoulding, and not only those who have not changed their basic stand; everybody should study and remould himself. I say "everybody", and this includes us who are present here. Conditions are changing all the time, and to adapt one's thinking to the new conditions, one must study. Even those who have a better grasp of Marxism and are comparatively firm in their proletarian stand have to go on studying, have to absorb what is new and tackle new problems. Unless they rid their minds of what is unsound, intellectuals cannot undertake the task of educating others. Naturally, we have to learn while teaching and be pupils while serving as teachers. To be a good teacher, one must first be a good pupil. There are many things which cannot be learned from books alone; one must learn from those engaged in production, from the workers, from the poor and lower middle peasants and, in schools, from the students, from those one teaches. In my opinion, the majority of our intellectuals are willing to learn. It is our task to help them warm-heartedly and in a proper way on the basis of their willingness to study; we must not resort to compulsion and force them to study.

Fourthly, there is the question of the integration of the intellectuals with the masses of workers and peasants. Since their task is to serve the masses of workers and peasants, the intellectuals must, first and foremost, know them and be familiar with their life, work and ideas. We encourage the intellectuals to go among the masses, to go to factories and villages. It is very bad if you never in all your life meet a worker or a peasant. Our government workers, writers, artists, teachers and scientific research workers should seize every opportunity to get close to the workers and peasants. Some can go to factories or villages just to look around; this may be called "looking at the flowers while on horseback" and is better than nothing at all. Others can stay there for a few months, conducting investigations and making friends; this may be called "dismounting to look at the flowers". Still others can stay and live there for a considerable time, say, two or three years or even longer; this may be called "settling down". Some intellectuals do live among the workers and peasants, for instance, the industrial technicians in factories and the agricultural technicians and rural school teachers in the countryside. They should do their work well and integrate themselves with the workers and peasants. We should create an atmosphere in which "getting close to the workers and peasants" virtually becomes a habit, in other words, we should have large numbers of intellectuals doing so. Not all of them of course; some are unable to go for one reason or another, but we hope that as many as possible will go. They cannot all go at the same time, but they can go in batches at different times. In the old days when we were in Yenan, the intellectuals were enabled to make direct contact with the workers and peasants. Many of them in Yenan were very confused in their thinking and came out with all sorts of queer arguments. We held a forum, advising them to go among the masses. Later many went, and the results were very good. Until an intellectual's book knowledge is integrated with practice, it is not complete, and it may be very incomplete indeed. It is chiefly through reading books that intellectuals acquire the experience of our predecessors. Of course, it is necessary to read books, but by itself it does not solve problems. One must study the actual situation, examine practical experience and concrete material, and make friends with the workers and peasants. Making friends with the workers and peasants is no easy job. Even now when people go to factories or villages, the results are good in some cases but not in others. What is involved here is the question of stand or attitude, that is, of one's world outlook. We advocate "letting a hundred schools of thought contend", and in every branch of learning there may be many schools and trends; in the matter of world outlook, however, today there are basically only two schools, the proletarian and the bourgeois. It is one or the other, either the proletarian or the bourgeois world outlook. The communist world outlook is the world outlook of the proletariat and of no other class. Most of our present intellectuals come from the old society and from families of non-working people. Even those who come from workers' or peasants' families are still bourgeois intellectuals because the education they received before liberation was a bourgeois education and their world outlook was fundamentally bourgeois. If they do not discard the old and replace it by the proletarian world outlook, they will remain different from the workers and peasants in their viewpoint, stand and feelings, and will be like square pegs in round holes, and the workers and peasants will not open

149

their hearts to them. If the intellectuals integrate themselves with the workers and peasants and make friends with them, the Marxism they have learned from books can become truly their own. In order to have a real grasp of Marxism, one must learn it not only from books, but mainly through class struggle, through practical work and close contact with the masses of workers and peasants. When in addition to reading some Marxist books our intellectuals have gained some understanding through close contact with the masses of workers and peasants and through their own practical work, we will all be speaking the same language, not only the common language of patriotism and the common language of the socialist system, but probably even the common language of the communist world outlook. If that happens, all of us will certainly work much better.

Fifthly, there is rectification. Rectification means correcting one's way of thinking and style of work. Rectification movements were conducted within the Communist Party during the anti-Japanese war, during the War of Liberation, and in the early days after the founding of the People's Republic of China.[2] Now the Central Committee of the Communist Party has decided on another rectification within the Party to be started this year. Non-Party people may take part in it, or they need not if they do not wish to. The main thing in this rectification movement is to criticize the following three errors in one's way of thinking and style of work — subjectivism, bureaucracy and sectarianism. As in the rectification movement in the anti-Japanese war, the method this time will be first to study a number of documents, and then, on the basis of such study, to examine one's own thinking and work and unfold criticism and self-criticism to expose shortcomings and mistakes and promote what is right and good. On the one hand, we must be strict and conduct criticism and self-criticism of mistakes and shortcomings seriously, and not perfunctorily, and correct them; on the other hand, we must not be rough but must follow the principle of "learning from past mistakes to avoid future ones and curing the sickness to save the patient", and we must oppose the method of "finishing people off with a single blow".

Ours is a great Party, a glorious Party, a correct Party. This must be affirmed as a fact. But we still have shortcomings, and this, too, must be affirmed as a fact. We should not affirm everything, but only what is correct; at the same time, we should not negate everything, but only what is wrong. Our achievements are the main thing in our work, and yet there are not a few shortcomings and mistakes. That is why we need a rectification movement. Will it undermine our Party's prestige if we criticize our own subjectivism, bureaucracy and sectarianism? I think not. On the contrary, it will serve to enhance our Party's prestige. The rectification movement during the anti-Japanese war proved this. It enhanced the prestige of our Party, of our Party comrades and our veteran cadres, and it also enabled the new cadres to make great progress. Which of the two was afraid of criticism, the Communist Party or the Kuomintang? The Kuomintang. It prohibited criticism, but that did not save it from final defeat. The Communist Party does not fear criticism because we are Marxists, the truth is on our side, and the basic masses, the workers and peasants, are on our side. As we used to say, the rectification movement is "a widespread movement of Marxist education".[3] Rectification means the whole Party studying Marxism through criticism and self-criticism. We can certainly learn more about Marxism in the course of the rectification movement.

The transformation and construction of China depend on us for leadership. When we have rectified our way of thinking and style of work, we shall enjoy greater initiative in our work, become more capable and work better. Our country has need of many people who whole-heartedly serve the masses and the cause of socialism and who are determined to bring about changes. We Communists should all be people of this kind. In old China it was a crime to talk about reforms, and offenders would be beheaded or imprisoned. Nevertheless there were determined reformers who, fearing nothing, published books and newspapers, educated and organized the people and waged indomitable struggles under every kind of difficulty. The people's democratic dictatorship has paved the way for the rapid economic and cultural development of our country. It is only a few years since the establishment of our state, and yet people can already see the unprecedented flowering of the economy, culture, education and science. In building up the new China we Communists are not daunted by any difficulties whatsoever. But we cannot accomplish this on our own. We need a good number of non-Party people with great ideals who will fight dauntlessly together with us for the transformation and construction of our society in the direction of socialism and communism. It is an arduous task to ensure a better life for the several hundred million people of China and to build our economically and culturally backward country into a prosperous and powerful one with a high level of culture. Therefore, in order to be able to shoulder this task more competently and work better together with all non-Party people who are actuated by high ideals and determined to institute reforms, we must conduct rectification movements both now and in the future, and constantly rid ourselves of whatever is wrong. Thorough-going materialists are fearless; we hope that all our fellow fighters will courageously shoulder their responsibilities and overcome all difficulties, fearing no setbacks or gibes, nor hesitating to criticize us Communists and give us their suggestions. "He who is not afraid of death by a thousand cuts dares to unhorse the emperor" — this is the indomitable spirit needed in our struggle to build socialism and communism. On our part, we Communists should create conditions helpful to those who co-operate with us, establish good comradely relations with them in our common work and unite with them in our joint struggle.

Sixthly, there is the question of one-sidedness. One-sidedness means thinking in terms of absolutes, that is, a metaphysical approach to problems. In the appraisal of our work, it is one-sided to regard everything either as all positive or as all negative. There are quite a few people inside the Communist Party and very many outside it who do just that. To regard everything as positive is to see only the good and not the bad, and to tolerate only praise and no criticism. To talk as though our work is good in every respect is at variance with the facts. It is not true that everything is good; there are still shortcomings and mistakes. But neither is it true that everything is bad, and that, too, is at variance with the facts. We must analyse things concretely. To negate everything is to think, without having made any analysis, that nothing has been done well and that the great work of socialist construction, the great struggle in which hundreds of millions of people are participating, is a complete mess with nothing in it worth commending. Although there is a difference between the many people who hold such views and those who are hostile to the socialist system, these views are very mistaken and harmful and can only dishearten people. It is wrong to appraise our work either from the viewpoint that everything is positive, or from the viewpoint that everything is negative. We should criticize those people who take such a one-sided approach to problems, though of course in criticizing them we should help them, keeping to the principle of "learning from past mistakes to avoid future ones and curing the sickness to save the patient".

Some people say: Since there is to be a rectification movement and since everyone is to be asked to express his opinions, one-sidedness is unavoidable, and therefore in calling for the elimination of one-sidedness, it seems that you really don't want people to speak up. Is this assertion right? It is naturally difficult for everyone to avoid any trace of one-sidedness. People always examine and handle problems and express their views in the light of their own experience, and unavoidably they sometimes show a little one-sidedness. However, should we not ask them gradually to overcome their one-sidedness and to look at problems in a relatively all-sided way? In my opinion, we should. Otherwise, we would be stagnating; we would be approving one-sidedness and contradicting the whole purpose of rectification if we did not make the demand that, from day to day and from year to year, more and more people should view problems in a relatively all-sided way. One-sidedness is a violation of dialectics. We want gradually to disseminate dialectics, and to ask everyone gradually to learn the use of the scientific dialectical method. Some of the articles now being published are extremely pompous but devoid of any content, any analysis of problems and any reasoned argument, and they carry no conviction. There should be fewer and fewer of such articles. When writing an article, one should not be thinking all the time, "How brilliant I am!" but should regard one's readers as on a completely equal footing with oneself. You may have been in the revolution for a long time, but all the same if you say something wrong, people will refute you. The more airs you put on, the less people will stand for it and the less they will care to read your articles. We should do our work honestly, analyse things concretely, write articles that carry conviction and never overawe people by striking a pose.

Some people say that while one-sidedness can be avoided in a lengthy article, it is unavoidable in a short essay. Must a short essay always be one-sided? As I have just said, it is usually hard to avoid one-sidedness and there is nothing terrible if a certain amount creeps in. Criticism would be hampered if everyone were required to look at problems in an absolutely all-sided way. Nevertheless we do ask everyone to try to approach problems in a relatively all-sided way and try to avoid one-sidedness in both long and short articles, short essays included. Some people argue, how is it possible to undertake analysis in an essay of a few hundred or one to two thousand words? I say, why not? Didn't Lu Hsun do it? The analytical method is dialectical. By analysis, we mean analysing the contradictions in things. And sound analysis is impossible without intimate knowledge of life and without real understanding of the pertinent contradictions. Lu Hsun's later essays are so penetrating and powerful and yet so free from one-sidedness precisely because he had grasped dialectics by then. Some of Lenin's articles can also be called short essays; they are satirical and pungent, but without one-sidedness. Almost all of Lu Hsun's essays were directed at the enemy; some of Lenin's essays were directed at the enemy and others at comrades. Can the Lu Hsun type of essay be used against mistakes and shortcomings within the ranks of the people? I think it can. Of course, we must make a distinction between the enemy and ourselves, and we must not adopt an antagonistic stand towards comrades and treat them as we would the enemy. In speaking up, one must have an ardent desire to protect the cause of the people and raise their political consciousness, and there must be no ridiculing or attacking in one's approach.

What if one dare not write? Some people say they dare not write even when they have something to say, lest they should offend people and be criticized. I think such worries can be cast aside. Ours is a democratic people's government, and it provides an environment conducive to writing in the service of the people. The policy of "letting a hundred flowers blossom and a hundred schools of thought contend" offers additional guarantees for the flowering of science and the arts. If what you say is right, you need fear no criticism, and you can explain your correct views further through debate. If what you say is wrong, then criticism can help you correct your mistakes, and there is nothing bad in that. In our society, militant revolutionary criticism and counter-criticism are the healthy method used to expose and resolve contradictions, develop science and the arts and ensure success in all our work.

Seventhly, to "open wide" or to "restrict"? This is a question of policy. "Let a hundred flowers blossom and a hundred schools of thought contend" is a long-term as well as a fundamental policy; it is not just a temporary policy. In the discussion, comrades expressed disapproval of "restriction", and I think this view is the correct one. The Central Committee of the Party is of the opinion that we must "open wide", not "restrict".

In leading our country, two alternative methods, or in other words two alternative policies, can be adopted — to "open wide" or to "restrict". To "open wide" means to let all people express their opinions freely, so that they dare to speak, dare to criticize and dare to debate; it means not being afraid of wrong views and anything poisonous; it means to encourage argument and criticism among people holding different views, allowing freedom both for criticism and for counter-criticism; it means not suppressing wrong views but convincing people by reasoning with them. To "restrict" means to forbid people to air differing opinions and express wrong ideas, and to "finish them off with a single blow" if they do so. That is the way to aggravate rather than to resolve contradictions. To "open wide", or to "restrict" — we must choose one or the other of these two policies. We choose the former, because it is the policy which will help to consolidate our country and develop our culture.

We are prepared to use the policy of "opening wide" to unite with the several million intellectuals and change their present outlook. As I have said above, the overwhelming majority of the intellectuals in our country want to make progress and remould themselves, and they are quite capable of remoulding themselves. In this connection, the policy we adopt will play a tremendous role. The question of the intellectuals is above all one of ideology, and it is not helpful but harmful to resort to crude and high-handed measures for solving ideological questions. The remoulding of the intellectuals, and especially the changing of their world out-look, is a process that requires a long period of time. Our comrades must understand that ideological remoulding in-volves long-term, patient and painstaking work, and they must not attempt to change people's ideology, which has been shaped over decades of life, by giving a few lectures or by holding a few meetings. Persuasion, not compulsion, is the only way to convince them. Compulsion will never result in convincing them. To try to convince them by force simply won't work. This kind of method is permissible in dealing with the enemy, but absolutely impermissible in dealing with comrades or friends. What if we don't know how to convince others? Then we have to learn. We must learn to conquer erroneous ideas through debate and reasoning.

"To let a hundred flowers blossom" is the way to develop the arts, and "to let a hundred schools of thought contend" is the way to develop science. Not only is this policy a good method of developing science and the arts, but, if given extended application, it constitutes a good method of doing all our work. It can help us to make fewer mis-takes. There are many things we don't understand and are therefore unable to tackle, but through debate and struggle we shall come to understand them and learn how to tackle them. Truth develops through debate between different views. The same method can be adopted with regard to whatever is poisonous and anti-Marxist, because Marxism will develop in the struggle against it. This is development through the struggle of opposites, development conforming to dialectics.

Haven't people discussed the true, the good and the beautiful all through the ages? Their opposites are the false, the evil and the ugly. The former would not exist without the latter. Truth stands in opposition to falsehood. In society as in nature, every entity invariably breaks up into its different parts, only there are differences in content and form under different concrete conditions. There will always be false and ugly phenomena. There will always be such opposites as the right and the wrong, the good and the evil, the beautiful and the ugly. The same is true of fragrant flowers and poisonous weeds. The relationship between them is one of the unity and struggle of opposites. There can be no differentiation without contrast. There can be no development without differentiation and struggle. Truth develops through its struggle against falsehood. This is how Marxism develops. Marxism develops in the struggle against bourgeois and petty-bourgeois ideology, and it is only through struggle that it can develop.

We are for the policy of "opening wide"; so far there has been too little of it rather than too much. We must not be afraid of opening wide, nor should we be afraid of criticism and poisonous weeds. Marxism is scientific truth; it fears no criticism and cannot be defeated by criticism. The same holds for the Communist Party and the People's Government; they fear no criticism and cannot be defeated by it. There will always be some things that are wrong, and that is nothing to be afraid of. Recently, a number of ghosts and monsters have been presented on the stage. Seeing this, some comrades have become very worried. In my opinion, a little of this does not matter much; within a few decades such ghosts and monsters will disappear from the stage altogether and you won't be able to see them even if you want to. We must promote what is right and oppose what is wrong, but we must not be frightened if people come in contact with erroneous things. It will solve no problem simply to issue administrative orders forbidding people to have any contact with perverse and evil phenomena and with erroneous ideas, or forbidding them to see ghosts and monsters on the stage. Of course, I am not advocating the spread of such things, I only say "a few of them do not matter much". It is not at all strange that erroneous things should exist, nor should this give any cause for fear; indeed it will help people learn to struggle against them better. Even great storms are not to be feared. It is amid great storms that human society progresses.

In our country bourgeois and petty-bourgeois ideology, anti-Marxist ideology, will continue to exist for a long time. Basically, the socialist system has been established in our country. We have won the basic victory in transforming the ownership of the means of production, but we have not yet won complete victory on the political and ideological fronts. In the ideological field, the question of who will win in the struggle between the proletariat and the bourgeoisie has not been really settled yet. We still have to wage a protracted struggle against bourgeois and petty-bourgeois ideology. It is wrong not to understand this and to give up ideological struggle. All erroneous ideas, all poisonous weeds, all ghosts and monsters, must be subjected to criticism; in no circumstance should they be allowed to spread unchecked. However, the criticism should be fully reasoned, analytical and convincing, and never rough, bureaucratic, metaphysical or dogmatic.

For a long time now people have been levelling a lot of criticism at dogmatism. That is as it should be. But they often neglect to criticize revisionism. Both dogmatism and revisionism run counter to Marxism. Marxism must certainly advance; it must develop along with the development of practice and cannot stand still. It would become lifeless if it remained stagnant and stereotyped. However, the basic principles of Marxism must never be violated, or otherwise mistakes will be made. It is dogmatism to approach Marxism from a metaphysical point of view and to regard it as something rigid. It is revisionism to negate the basic principles of Marxism and to negate its universal truth. Revisionism is one form of bourgeois ideology. The revisionists deny the differences between socialism and capitalism, between the dictatorship of the proletariat and the dictatorship of the bourgeoisie. What they advocate is in fact not the socialist line but the capitalist line. In present circumstances, revisionism is more pernicious than dogmatism. One of our current important tasks on the ideological front is to unfold criticism of revisionism.

Eighthly and lastly, the Party committees of the provinces, municipalities and autonomous regions must tackle the question of ideology. This is the point some of the comrades present here wanted me to touch upon. In many places, the Party committees have not yet tackled the question of ideology, or have done very little in this respect. The main reason is that they are busy. But they must tackle it. By "tackling it" I mean that it must be put on the agenda and studied. The large-scale, turbulent class struggles of the masses characteristic of the previous revolutionary periods have in the main come to an end, but there is still class struggle — mainly on the political and ideological fronts — and it is very acute too. The question of ideology has now become very important. The first secretaries of the Party committees in all localities should personally tackle this question, which can be solved correctly only when they have given it serious attention and gone into it. All localities should call meetings on propaganda work, similar to our present one, to discuss local ideological work and all related problems. Such meetings should be attended not only by Party comrades but also by people outside the Party, and moreover by people with different opinions. This is all to the good and no harm can come of it, as the experience of the present meeting has proved.

NOTES

[1] The Chinese Communist Party's National Conference on Propaganda Work was held by the Central Committee of the Party in Peking from March 6 to 13, 1957. It was attended by more than 380 leading cadres of the Party's propaganda, cultural and educational departments at the central and provincial (or municipal) levels. Also, more than 100 non-Party people were invited from various departments and institutions of science, education, literature and art, and the press.

[2] The rectification movement during the anti-Japanese war was conducted in 1942 on a large scale in the Party organizations in Yenan and other anti-Japanese base areas to combat subjectivism, sectarianism and stereotyped writing. The rectification during the War of Liberation was a movement for Party consolidation, which was conducted extensively in the Party organizations in the Liberated Areas in 1948 in co-ordination with the land reform movement. The rectification in the early days after the founding of the People's Republic of China was conducted throughout the Party in 1950 after nation-wide victory, with the aim of intensifying education among the large numbers of new Party members and changing their impure ideology, and of overcoming complacency and a commandist style of work among old Party members which began to grow as a result of victory.

[3] See "On Production by the Army for Its Own Support and on the Importance of the Great Movements for Rectification and for Production", *Selected Works of Mao Tse-tung*, Eng. ed., FLP, Peking, 1965, Vol. III, pp. 325-29.

毛泽东论文学和艺术

*

外文出版社出版（北京）
1960年第一版
1967年第三版
（译文修订本）
编号：（英）1050—105
00062
1—E—418P